the Perfect Omelet

the Perfect Omelet

ESSENTIAL RECIPES
FOR THE HOME COOK

John E. Finn

THE COUNTRYMAN PRESS
A DIVISION OF W. W. NORTON & COMPANY
Independent Publishers Since 1923

Manufacturing by Versa Press
Book design by Seton Rossini
Production manager: Devon Zahn

Library of Congress Cataloging-in-Publication Data

Names: Finn, John E., author.
Title: The perfect omelet : essential recipes for the home cook / John E. Finn.
Description: New York, NY : Countryman Press, a division of W. W. Norton & Company, Independent Publishers Since 1923, [2017] | Includes bibliographical references and index.
Identifiers: LCCN 2016055404 | ISBN 9781581573664 (hardcover)
Subjects: LCSH: Omelets. | LCGFT: Cookbooks.
Classification: LCC TX745 .F56 2017 | DDC 641.6/75—dc23 LC record available at https://lccn.loc.gov/2016055404

33614080186629

The Countryman Press
www.countrymanpress.com

A division of W. W. Norton & Company, Inc.
500 Fifth Avenue, New York, NY 10110
www.wwnorton.com

10 9 8 7 6 5 4 3 2 1

For Linda

*We do not find the meaning of life by
ourselves alone—we find it with another.*

—THOMAS MERTON

Contents

Introduction: The Perfect Omelet

Be content to remember that those who can make
omelettes properly can do nothing else.

—HILAIRE BELLOC, *A CONVERSATION WITH A CAT*

This is not a sad story:

I am alone in my kitchen. In front of me is my mother's yellow omelet pan. It is nice to look at, even cute, but at 6 inches in diameter and with impossibly steep sides, it is impracticable if not useless.

I should put the pan in the Goodwill box, along with all the other small gimcracks I have come upon in the months after my mother died from lung cancer (two packs a day for 40 years. She said it was a fair trade). But I can't say good-bye.

Without thinking, I set the pan on the stove and anoint it with butter. I crack two brown eggs and add a bit of water, salt, and pepper. Precisely three drops of Tabasco. With a fork, I bring the eggs to a furious froth and wait for the butter to bubble. Two minutes pass and the result matches my mood and the pan. Beaten into submission, the eggs are bruised and tough. And I can't convince the omelet onto the plate; it sits there in the pan, sullen, stubborn, and uncooperative. (Oh no! Mom has been reincarnated as an omelet!) I should be disappointed, but instead I am cross, not with the omelet, not with myself, but with my mother. It is, after all, her pan. It is her recipe as well. It is her fault.

Nevertheless, it is my omelet, by my hand, and I know that somewhere my mother is laughing, really laughing, amused by my mistake. (She would call it, and me, a foozle.) I haven't heard her laugh in many years, not since my father widowed her, but I can hear her now. I settle into a smile, and relinquish the eggs to Daisy, my mother's Boston terrier, who has been waiting at my feet. (Daisy came with the pan.) Can a dog be smug? Daisy, too, might be a candidate for the good-bye box . . .

My mother was obsessed with omelets. She would skip and chirp about, "as happy as a lark," as she would say, when she came across a newspaper recipe advising the amateur chef to add a drop or two (maybe three) of Tabasco. (I can still see the clipping in my mind's eye, but I wish I had the piece of paper she cut out and stored in her little wooden box.) She stayed happy, if not jubilant, for a few months or so, or however long it took her to unearth yet another secret (add water, not milk; clarify the butter; or my favorite: use only *brown* eggs) for making the perfect omelet.

My mom's obsession with omelets sometimes embarrassed me. She snuck into the kitchen once at a new restaurant in Seattle (was it called Eggs Etc.? The Omelet Factory? I can't recall) that specialized in omelets, intent on asking the chef about some finer point of omeletry (omeleting?). I sat alone, small at the table, hoping she wouldn't be arrested. I don't know what she learned on her uninvited tour of the back of the house, but we never ate there again. I still imagine her photograph on a Do Not Admit poster by the door. She panned my choice of restaurant for the all-important senior prom dinner because its frittatas were not up to her standards. (I wasn't thinking about the food, much less about frittatas. Neither was my date, thus confirming my mother's disappointment.) We ate instead at a local seafood place. I cannot recall whether the menu included a Clam Omelet Normande (clams, chives, juniper berries, and sauce normande), but I would have chosen something less daunting.

My mother was an earnest and accomplished cook, particularly adept at cheesecakes (and omelets), though curiously inept at meat loaf and pot roast. You might surmise, then, that I learned how to make the perfect omelet from my mother.

In a fashion. I did not realize it then, but my mother made me Sancho Panza to her quest for the perfect omelet. (She and my father loved the Broadway musicals of the 1950s and 1960s. It wasn't Sunday morning without a musical on my father's prized Fisher hi-fi.) Thinking about it now, I was a poor, inattentive, and uninterested *chef de tournant* (relief cook). In my defense, I was young and did not come to realize how important an omelet is until I was older and wiser.

What I *did* learn about omelets (and pretty much about everything else) from my mother is this: There is no secret recipe for the perfect omelet. A perfect omelet does not have a canonical look or form. It cannot be reduced to a formula or mass-produced in a factory. A perfect omelet is not a thing to be admired and consumed. The perfect omelet is a *way* of doing things, a philosophy about how to cook and, mayhap, about how to live.

If that sounds pretentious or intimidating, remember that a philosophy is simply a way to be in the world, a way of conducting one's life. Indeed, in many philosophical traditions (the Stoics, to take one prominent example, and the Epicureans, for another, notwithstanding their seemingly contradictory precepts), "philosophy did not consist in teaching an abstract theory . . . but rather in the art of living." Philosophies, understood this way, are lessons in how to live. Moreover, philosophy tells us there is no single way to live a life good and true, much less one we can learn from a book. Philosophy asks us to think for ourselves, to find our own way, our own voice. Philosophy is a way of being in the world that prizes questions more than answers, that takes joy in exploration and finds meaning in experience. Not just about matters abstract and ephemeral (like how to live) but also about matters concrete and quotidian (such as how to cook).

A Philosophy of Omelets & Cooking

What is true of philosophy is true of omelets. It cannot be an accident that the traditional shape of the fabled philosopher's stone is that of an egg. There is a philosophy in an egg (or, rather, as Ezra Pound notes, in its yolk) and likewise a philosophy implicit in the search for a perfect omelet.

The Perfect Omelet embraces a philosophy of cooking that rejects the idea that there is a perfect recipe for anything, one that will guarantee a perfect result, every time, if only we will do as we are told. A perfect omelet is not a matter of reading a recipe but a way of doing, a way of cooking. Cooking, like philosophy, "is the transforming of the half-intuited into the fully conceived, a working over and making digestible for others."

It is easy enough to understand why my mother searched so long for the perfect recipe: The idea of failing scared her. She wanted to get things right. Moreover, what it meant to get things right was caught up with what it meant to be a good mother, a good wife, a good friend, and a good host. Early on, she believed she could make things perfect, for herself, for her family, for her friends, if only she could find just the right technique, a secret trick . . . or the perfect recipe.

It is not difficult to find recipes that promise perfection.

In "Omelets Revisited," a recipe from a 1993 issue of *Cook's Illustrated*, we learn there are "four steps to a perfect omelet," and all of them are about technique and tools. Formerly the handiwork only of a "trained chef, or at least a very serious cook," omelets are now a "cinch," provided one follows directions and has a good nonstick pan. A more recent version (2009) of the perfect omelet, also in *Cook's Illustrated*, is far more complicated, requiring the cook to freeze little pieces of butter, to separate eggs, to beat them for "about 80 strokes," and then to use chopsticks or wooden skewers to move the eggs in the pan. Following each step religiously leads, presumably, to a perfect omelet. In his masterful compendium, *Egg: A Culinary Exploration of the World's Most Versatile Ingredient*, Michael Ruhlman includes an entire section entitled "How to Make a Perfect Omelet." It is chock-full of good advice and, equally important, brutally honest, advising us that a perfect omelet "takes practice," and that "errors are glaring."

A perfect recipe appeals to us precisely because, unlike Ruhlman's honest account, it promises success. Such a recipe relieves us of a certain kind of anxiety, what some have called, facetiously, "Kitchen Performance Anxiety Syndrome." Performance anxiety may seem far-fetched to confident cooks, but for many of us there is indeed an apprehension associated with cooking—an anxiety occasioned not only by the prospect of failing, but also by having to make choices about what to purchase, how to prepare it, and how to serve it. Anxious cooks are the sorts of cooks who, when confronted with a recipe that calls for a specific ingredient they do not have or cannot find, will forgo the recipe altogether rather than substitute or experiment with something else (unless the recipe tells them they can!).

A perfect recipe offers an escape from the necessity and weight of having to make and accept responsibility for independent choices and decisions. Even M. F. K. Fisher once wrote, "as a spoilt idiot-child of the twentieth-century, I want to be told." We all want to be told, but the study of philosophy teaches us that to be fully human—to be free—is to think and to do for ourselves. When we cook from blind obedience, without thinking, we embrace what Joanne Finkelstein has called "a kind of incivility," or an inability to reflect and examine "what constitutes the good life." People who follow recipes blindly or who work to "someone else's set of rules, word for word," never realize "there is more to cooking than obediently following a recipe." To live without thinking, and to cook without thinking, is to be less than free, less than fully human.

It may seem curious, if not ironic, but our pursuit of perfection requires failure. Every time we try to find our own way, we risk getting lost. Every time we cook, we risk a foozle, as my mother might say. This is especially so when the dish at hand, like an omelet, seems complicated and intricate. And let's be honest: An omelet seems complicated and intricate because it *is*. A perfect omelet, or at least the quintessential French omelet, requires just the right mix of eggs and butter, a pan that is not too big or too small, not too hot and not too cold. It must be cooked not a second too long, lest it become something else, something pedestrian, ordinary, like scrambled eggs. (Apologies to Auguste Escoffier, who once described scrambled eggs as "undoubtedly the finest of all egg preparations.") When prepared properly, however, an omelet is a radiant, shimmering golden gift from heaven, creamy on the inside, graced by an outer layer of egg with the consistency and firmness of lace.

There is no single, indisputably correct way to make such an omelet.

Indeed, there are so many right ways to omelet (an omelet is not simply a meal, it is a verb) that a novice might reasonably think it is safer to scramble. Like life itself, the omelet is something of a mystery, as ordinary as breakfast and as profound as Plato. Achieving omelet perfection is indeed difficult. But as John Ciardi reminds us, "the word 'difficult' [is] not one to be afraid of." There is, he writes, "a pleasure in taking pains." A perfect omelet takes practice and patience; mistakes are a common if not the probable outcome. (Happily, the "mistakes are delicious.")

On the other hand, failure, at least with omelets, is easy enough to avoid, if one really wants to. You do not need a perfect recipe to avoid calamity. Once reserved to a chef with a practiced hand and a prized pan, omelets have become another victim of kitchen technology. Instant omelets (just add water!) were among the first convenience foods, featured prominently at the New York World's Fair in 1964. Frozen omelets, wrapped like Band-Aids and just as tasty, are a staple in supermarkets and require only a minute in a microwave. Sadly, not even France has had the courage to make these faux-omelets illegal, perhaps because there are other, more horrific crimes against omelets. One such felony is the Ziploc omelet, which requires only eggs, a pot of boiling water, and, of course, a Ziploc bag.

Omelet *mécanique,* moreover, has given us pans with hinges that fold and which require no more artistry than the ability to crack an egg and turn the pan upside down, sort of like those countertop waffle makers we have all tried at the hotel. (Yes, it is quite possible to use a waffle iron to make something you can call an omelet. I can't believe my mother never tried it.) Among my collection of many omelet contraptions is an "Omelet in a Pot" apparatus that uses a similar principle to make omelets in a microwave. I have seen versions that promise perfect omelets in less than two minutes and which retail for nearly $20. Another, called "Omelet Ease," comes complete with a peculiar-looking plastic egg face at the end of the handle that locks and unlocks the hinges. (For a modest sum, you can purchase a special spatula with the same odd decoration.) Fancier and costlier versions by Calphalon and other prestigious manufacturers routinely show up in my Williams-Sonoma and Sur La Table catalogs.

But if technology has given us omelets in a baggie and gimmickry masquerading as cookware, it has also given us nonstick pans and heat resistant spatulas, as well as thousands of internet recipes and instructional videos on YouTube. A mindful cook can find organic, free-range eggs, local herbs, and fresh farmer's cheeses. Once a private enterprise, the province of professionals at the hotel brunch bar (unlike the waffle station, the omelet station, you will have noticed, is staffed by a chef in a starched white coat), fine omelets are now a broadly democratic affair, accessible to anyone who wants to try and is willing to fail in the quest for perfection.

What Is a Perfect Omelet?

All of which begs the question: What is a perfect omelet?

Fearsome, French, and fussy, omelets intimidate many cooks. Mastering one is the mark of an accomplished chef. As a fifteen-year-old apprentice, a frustrated Pierre Franey threw his attempt at an Omelette aux fines herbes at the sous-chef at the Restaurant Drouant in Paris. By his own admission, Franey's omelet was an inferior specimen in every way: wrinkly, crinkly, and brown. I remember trembling in anxiety at the prospect of having to cook the same omelet for Chef André Soltner, then recently retired from Lutèce and newly installed as Dean éminence grise at the culinary school I attended. I practiced for days on end, and not once produced a credible omelet. There is no happy end to this story, no tale of triumph in the face of uncertainty and self-doubt. I did cook an omelet for Chef Soltner. He was kind, gentle, and forgiving. After consulting with my mother (I am sure), Soltner said nothing and moved on to the next unworthy student. Somewhere in omelet hell, my omelet sits cold and shriveled, in silent shameful company with Franey's failure.

So, what is a perfect omelet? There is no lack of advice about how to cook the perfect omelet, and plenty of disagreement about what *per-*

fect means. Consider the following ways in which we might think an omelet, or a recipe, is "perfect."

A recipe might be perfect because it always works. *Perfect*, in other words, might refer to how a dish is prepared, or to aspects of technique. The recipe is perfect because, provided one can follow directions, any cook, no matter how skilled or inexpert, is sure to get the right result. Following each step religiously leads to a perfect omelet. This is the logic of the two recipes from *Cook's Illustrated*.

Ordinarily, these recipes are quite detailed if not needlessly complicated. They tend to be insistent that the only sure way to success comes from following directions closely and without digression. The cook who will not do as she is told is worse than a nonconformist: That cook is certain to fail. That said, technique matters, not only in omeletry, but in cooking at large. As Michael Ruhlman has preached repeatedly, "the world is awash in recipes. . . . But if you know a single technique, you immediately have hundreds of recipes at hand."

Alternatively, a recipe may be perfect because it promises an authentic result. An omelet recipe might be perfect because it is a "true" or faithful representation of what it signifies, or a "matter of authentic preparation." A recipe might be perfect because it yields a reasonable facsimile of the iconic French version of the omelet: perfectly pale and perfectly creamy. Often such recipes insist that the cook track down ingredients that originate from and are unique to a certain place, or which are "genuine," or which are prepared only in certain ways (and, according to some folks, only by certain people!).

A recipe might also be perfect along a dimension of taste. What does it mean to say that a recipe is perfect because the food tastes good? We might regard the query as a physiological claim (This "tastes good.") and thus ask, "Is anything about gustatory taste universal"? Is there some measure or standard against which we can assess how good something tastes, or how nearly it approaches perfection? The familiar aphorism "De gustibus non est disputandum" seems to suggest not. We all know taste is personal, idiosyncratic, and subjective, and as Proust reminds us, prejudiced by memory and emotion.

Alternatively, and of equal importance to philosophers and to cooks alike, "perfect taste" might be a claim about aesthetics ("This is in good taste.") In any recipe, some element of taste is irreducibly physiological, but the larger part is about appearance—taste is always visual as well as physiological. Seeing isn't believing. Seeing is *tasting*. We find this sort of assessment in Mark Bittman's review of the "perfect omelet" recipe from *Cook's Illustrated* that we mentioned earlier: "It was the perfect consistency—light, fluffy and gorgeous."

So, a recipe might be perfect in several different ways, perhaps regarding reliability, or authenticity, or taste. It may not be obvious, but all these definitions embody a philosophy, or a way of thinking about cooking, in which the recipe controls and directs us to chop, sizzle, stir, simmer, and coddle in a certain way, and only that way, in return for a guarantee of success. There is a high price to pay for this sort of perfection. These recipes encourage us to cook without comprehension or reflection.

When we cook from blind obedience, we cook without thinking. Like Charles Dickens's Bitzer, who can define a horse but knows nothing of horses, we learn nothing about the dish itself, and hence nothing about cooking or about ourselves. Insofar as they insist upon conformity rather than creativity and confidence, it is not much of an exaggeration to say that perfect recipes make good meals and bad cooks. As chef-critic Daniel Patterson observes, "Cookbooks should teach us how to cook, not just follow instructions. . . . The point of a recipe should be to help us find our own way." Recipes that promise perfection make no effort to teach. They simply tell us where to go and how to get there. *The Perfect Omelet*, borrowing from my mother, rejects that way of cooking.

The Puzzled Omelet: Definitions and Distinctions

An astute reader may have noticed that my discussion of the perfect *recipe* has eluded the more important question: What is a perfect *omelet*? An omelet might be perfect in different ways and for lots of reasons. It might taste good. It might look nice. It might bear a fair resemblance to something French. We might say an omelet is the perfect quick breakfast, the perfect light lunch, the perfect elegant dinner, and even the perfect distinctive desert! But what makes an omelet truly perfect? Narcissa Chamberlain, as familiar with the nuances of omelets as anyone, supposed that a "perfect one *aux fines herbes* may be the true pinnacle" of omeletdom. A more democratic view is that only you can decide. In the words of Elizabeth David, "there is only one infallible recipe for the perfect omelette: your own."

All you need is a place to start.

Definitions are a good place to start because they tell us nothing of genuine importance. The innumerable variety (of definitions and of omelets) tells us that an omelet is not a thing, but rather a collection of ideas organized casually around a way of thinking about and cooking eggs. An omelet is less an egg than an idea about an egg, and we cannot shutter an idea in a shell.

Can we be more precise? One of my favorite poets, Marilyn Hacker, describes the "Platonic ideal" omelet as "only hot, loose eggs at its heart, with fresh herbs." Another definition holds that all omelets are, "in their essence, the same: beaten eggs cooked in a skillet into a flat disk." Another connoisseur says an omelet "is a little like scrambled eggs (but not quite) folded into a sort of self-envelope."

These somewhat imprecise definitions raise questions that might trouble the thinking cook nearly as much as they trouble a figmental Jean-Paul Sartre in his fruitless search for an omelet that "expresses the meaninglessness of existence." What is an omelet, exactly? Is there a canonical list of required ingredients? No doubt, we can make an omelet with many *kinds* of eggs (ostrich eggs are delectable), and perhaps with just *parts* of an egg (think of egg white omelets), and maybe even with egg substitutes (shudder), but . . . Can we make an omelet *without* eggs? A Denver omelet without eggs is what? A sauté of ham, onions, and bell peppers?

Maybe an omelet is more a matter of technique, requiring a unique or distinctive manner of preparation. What is that technique? Even the iconic Omelette nature, we shall see, may be prepared in several different ways. Some chefs shake the pan and stir the eggs. Others move only the pan. Others only the egg. What is the difference, if any, between an omelet, a frittata, and a tortilla? (We take up this very question in Chapter 4, which concerns international omelets.) For that matter, what is the difference between an omelet and a scramble? Is a quiche an omelet? Is a soufflé an omelet? All of them use eggs, and there is an entire genus of omelet known as the soufflé omelet—indeed, there is an entire chapter in this book on soufflé omelets!

Philosophers love these kinds of questions, principally because no one knows the answers to them. Perhaps the definition of omelet is an example of what prominent Scottish philosopher Walter Bryce Gallie called an "essentially contested concept," one whose meaning and definition can be reasonably disagreed upon by reasonable people and which can be settled by no authority.

For now, I note only that many of these questions about definition lead inexorably to a topic of recurrent and profound concern among food scholars, chefs, and even diners: What makes an omelet (or any dish) "authentic"? The topic generates intense discussion and disagreement. There are those who hold to the view that some notion of authenticity is a vital part of preserving local foodways and of maintaining the dignity and autonomy of indigenous culinary traditions. We might regard laws, such as those in the European Union, that create PDOs (protected designation of origin), PGIs (protected geographical indication), and TSGs (traditional specialties guaranteed), as laudable efforts to protect the reputation and authenticity of local and regional foods. Just recently, for example, the European Union granted TSG status to Neapolitan pizza. Others argue that concerns about authenticity are misplaced if not pointless. Consider what one scholar has called "the ambiguity of authenticity." Is authenticity a matter of place? Of ingredients? Of timelessness? As Lisa Heldke asks: "What kind of authenticity is authentic"?

Always implicit in debates about authenticity are questions of power and politics: Who gets to decide what is authentic or inauthentic? In my view, concerns about authenticity usually say more about the consumer or the person concerned than they do about the "true" nature of the dish or the recipe. The right way to think about authenticity is to think less in terms of *fidelity* and more in terms of *respect*, not only for the dish and its ingredients, but also for the culture of its origin. This sort of respect is a crucial component of all good cooking: "Good cooking requires us to pay attention, to think, and to taste our food and evaluate it throughout the cooking process."

There is a case to make for paying attention. It sharpens the mind and deepens our appreciation. Almost paradoxically, our intense focus on what is in front of us is what enables us to see beyond ourselves and beyond the moment. This means that authenticity is not only about thoughtful cooking, it is also about mindful eating. Food "gets more authentic the more we occupy ourselves with it. . . . Authenticity is, in this sense a quality of eaters rather than one of the food eaten." In the words of culinary theologian Robert Farrar Capon, "Man's real work is to look at the things of the world and to love them for what they are. . . . It can cost him time and effort, but it pays handsomely."

How to Spell "Omelet"?

Having gone full existentialist, we might also ask aloud if there is a correct way to spell *omelet*. Is it spelled "omelet"? "omlt"? "omelette"? "ommellette"? (I have seen all of these and worse.) The website "Grammarist" notes that most American reference sources prefer *omelet*, whereas continental sources understandably favor the French *omelette*. The authoritative *Larousse Gastronomique* of course prefers the more elegant French spelling, while the equally authoritative and staid *Oxford English Dictionary* unsurprisingly prefers the more economical version.

One might sensibly ask: Who cares?

Well, I do. A little. There may not be a single, indisputably correct way to spell *omelet*, not any more than there is a single, indisputably correct way to make one, but surely, there are wrong ways. Respect for the omelet, for ourselves, and for others, asks that we make the effort to get things right. Like cooking, language is one of only a very few ways we have of reaching outside ourselves, for entering into communication, if not communion with others, past and present. The reason to spell *omelet* correctly—or at least to avoid the worst misspellings—is to nod in respect to others, to honor their cultural ways and mores, their history, their very identity. Neglecting to make that effort is a mark of disdain, a lack of regard for others. It makes us as haughty as Humpty-Dumpty:

> *"When I use a word," Humpty Dumpty said, in rather a scornful tone, "it means just what I choose it to mean—neither more nor less."*
>
> *"The question is," said Alice, "whether you can make words mean so many different things."*
>
> *"The question is," said Humpty Dumpty, "which is to be master—that's all."*

A Brief History of Omelets

The great surrealist artist Salvador Dalí shared my mother's obsession with omelets. Best known for his iconic melting clocks, Dalí composed several works dealing with "omelettes" in the 1930s, and on occasion carried an omelet in the pocket of his jacket. The master even autographed a half-eaten Cheddar omelet with a pink marker when approached by an admirer in a New York City restaurant!

Omelets have always been the object of someone's obsession. Indeed, there have been omelets nearly as long as there have been eggs. Some genealogies of the omelet trace it to a Roman dish, *ova mellita* (sometimes spelled *overmele*), recorded in one of history's first cookbooks, which consisted of eggs cooked on clay with honey and pepper. Another cookbook,

Le Ménagier, from late in the 14th century, has two recipes for *alumelles*, an early reference to flat omelets. A recipe from the 1400s for a dish called *froise* is in fact a recipe for a kind of bacon omelet; another is an omelet with chopped herbs, including tansy. We can find early recipes for a *frictata* (a precursor to the frittata) in a cookbook by Maestro Martino da Como, dated around 1450. The *frictata* sounds delicious, calling for eggs and grated cheese, as well as parsley, borage (sometimes called starflower), mint, marjoram, and sage.

Most authorities, however, locate the germinal omelet in a mid-16th-century French dish, *lemelle* or *alamelle* (meaning "small blade"—a key to the shape of a rolled omelet), which later became *alumette*, and finally *omelette*. Writing of meals in the court of Henry III, Thomas Artus describes an omelet "dusted with powdered musk, ambergris, and pearls." Ambergris, I'm sure you know, is a waxy, fragrant spice derived from the intestines of sperm whales (check your local market). La Varenne's *Le Patissier françois* (1653), the first French cookbook translated into English, includes several recipes for omelets, including a cream omelet that looks very much like a soufflé omelet, and farced (or stuffed) omelets. Other recipe collections from the 17th century include omelets that come near to contemporary ones, as well as some that seem strange by any measure.

By the late 19th century, recipes for "omelettes" were commonplace in European and American cookbooks. One of the most important of early American domestic cookbooks, for example, *Mrs. Beeton's Book of Household Management* (1892), contains nine, including recipes for both soufflé and sweet omelets. In contrast, Charles Ranhofer, the celebrated chef at Delmonico's, one of New York City's finest if not its first restaurant, included 48 recipes in his masterpiece of haute cuisine, *The Epicurean* (1894). Among them was an unusual Omelet Bonvalet, composed of mushrooms, marinated tuna fish, meat glaze, and cooked ham, and sauced with a classic espagnole (brown) sauce with minced gherkins.

Escoffier included 85 omelets in his *Guide to the Fine Art of French Cuisine* (1903). Many of Escoffier's recipes seem garish or excessive to contemporary tastes. An Omelette à la Rossini, for instance, calls for "two teaspoons foie gras and as much truffle" garnished with additional truffle and truffle essence. Escoffier's recipes were organized neatly and systematically. Similarly, *La Repertoire de Cuisine*, first published in 1914 and long a standard reference for professional chefs, has 75 recipes organized alphabetically. (One could argue that the comprehensive lists of omelets typically included in these collections best illustrates the systematization and organization of French haute cuisine in the 18th and 19th centuries.) Even these lists may be considered economical, if not perilously incomplete, when measured against later compilations. The authoritative *Larousse Gastronomique* (2001) identifies well over 75 varieties, and Roger Lallemand's *Les Omelettes* (1986) has nearly 150 recipes organized by the region in France from which they originate. *The Omelette Book* (1955), by Narcissa G. Chamberlain, indisputably the single best book on omelets and maybe on anything else, includes 300 recipes organized by technique and foodstuff. The late Madam Romaine de Lyon's (proprietor of the famous omelet bistro in New York City) book, *The Art of Cooking Omelettes* (1963), has no less than 500 recipes!

The Literary Omelet

The omelet likewise appears very early on in literary texts. The Orphic cults of Greece, for example, celebrate the omelet in the following verse from the sixth century BC:

> *O mighty first begotten,*
> *hear my prayer*
> *Two-fold, egg-born, and*
> *Wandering thru the air.*
> *Bull-roarer, glorying in thy golden wings,*
> *From whom the race of gods and mortals springs.*

We should not be surprised to learn that poets regard omelets with great affection. Indeed, some poems are both poems and recipes. In "Omelette," Marilyn Hacker advises:

> *First, chop an onion and sauté it separately*
> *In melted butter, unsalted, preferably.*

Add mushrooms (add girelles in autumn)
Stir until golden and gently wilted.
Then, break the eggs as neatly as possible,
crack! On the lip of the copper lip of the mixing bowl;
beat, frothing whites and yolks together,
thread with a filet of cream. You've melted
more butter in a scrupulous seven-inch
iron skillet: pour the mixture in swiftly, keep
flame high as edges puff and whiten.
Lower the flame to a reminiscence.

Jonathan Aaron's "Cooking an Omelet" is similarly a recipe for a two-egg omelet with fresh herbs and sometimes onions.

A recent work by Wally Swist, "Dinner with Camus," features a conversation with Albert Camus. The conversation ranges widely, including an exchange concerning Mersault's eggs in *L'Etranger*. An omelet features as part of a poetic riddle in "A Collegelands Catechism," by Paul Muldoon, winner of the 2003 Pulitzer Prize for poetry.

Perhaps because both poetry and omeletry satisfy the soul, many omelets have great (French) poets as their namesake. An Omelette Baudelaire, for instance, is made of sausage, tomato, peppers, garlic, parsley, and cheese. An Omelette André Theuriet requires morels, truffles, and asparagus, and an Omelette Jules Romains is composed of sausage, spinach, onion, rice, and fresh herbs. Ham, foie gras, mushrooms, truffles, walnuts, and cognac constitute an exceptionally rich Omelette Jean Cocteau. Just as rich and unusually complicated is an Omelette Jean Racine, composed of veal, lardons, spinach, mushrooms, and croutons. The mushrooms, lardons, veal, and cooked spinach are used to sauce the eggs. Sweetbreads are common in French omelets and the principal ingredient in an Omelette Paul Valéry, which includes also tomatoes, spinach, croutons, and cheese, in a sherry sauce. A fittingly romantic Omelette Victor Hugo includes beef, tomatoes, eggplant, noodles, garlic, and cheese.

Omelets, ordinary, elegant, and sometimes fanciful, figure prominently in popular literature and in the classics, as evidenced by Alice

B. Toklas's allusion to omelets as marks of social distinction in *The Alice B. Toklas Cook Book* (1954). Fans of Toklas will remember Hélène's calculated insult of the great Henri Matisse, announcing that she "will not make [him] an omelette but fry the eggs. It takes the same number of eggs and the same amount of butter but it shows less respect, and he will understand." The *Toklas* cookbook contains several recipes for omelets, including one inspired by an omelet George Sand sent to Victor Hugo, an Omelette Aurore, a sweet soufflé composed of candied fruits, marrons glacés, diced angelica, and macaroons. Other entries include a Tri-Coloured Omelette with spinach, saffron, and pureed tomatoes and the wonderfully named Omelette in an Overcoat, with mushrooms, spring onions, and shallots in a white sauce. (Is this where Dalí found the inspiration to carry one about in his jacket, presumably without the sauce?) The Omelette Sans Nom is a soufflé omelet with diced ham, a pinch of parmesan, and heavy cream.

In Alexandre Dumas *père*'s *Twenty Years After*, the musketeer D'Artagnan disparages an "omelet of Crevecoeur" as meager fare. I have been unable to locate a recipe for such an omelet (presumably, it includes Crevecoeur chicken, from Normandy) but Madame Romaine de Lyon includes in her book a recipe for an Omelette Alexandre Dumas, composed, surprisingly, not of chicken but of beef, lardons, carrots, peas, onions, and fines herbes. The Omelette Dumas recalls a long French tradition of naming omelets for prominent literary figures and public personalities. An Omelette Moliere [*sic*] includes beef, rice, and mushrooms, and an Omelette Balzac requires chicken, bacon, croutons, oyster plant, and cheese. A fine Omelette Jules Verne is composed of mushrooms, peas, Boston lettuce, croutons, and cream sauce.

Not many philosophers have omelet namesakes, but Rousseau and Voltaire, because they are French, are tasty exceptions. If it did not exist, it would be necessary to invent an Omelette Voltaire, composed of bacon, mushrooms, onion, croutons, and fines herbes. An Omelette Jean-Jacques Rousseau requires sausages, lardons, tomatoes, onions, and fines herbes, and likely will be my dinner this evening. Rousseau was so adept at omelets that he "could turn his beaten eggs by tossing them in the air, like a pancake." The fictional *Jean-Paul Sartre Cookbook* also includes several omelets, including a Denver omelet, but none that ever fulfill Sartre's greatest desire:

October 4

Still working on the omelet. There have been stumbling blocks. I keep creating omelets one after another, like soldiers marching into the sea, but each one seems empty, hollow, like stone. I want to create an omelet that expresses the meaninglessness of existence, and instead they taste like cheese. I look at them on the plate, but they do not look back. Tried eating them with the lights off. It did not help. Malraux suggested paprika.

October 6

I have realized that the traditional omelet form (eggs and cheese) is bourgeois. Today I tried making one out of a cigarette, some coffee, and four tiny stones. I fed it to Malraux, who puked. I am encouraged, but my journey is still long.

Perhaps my favorite honorific omelet, however, is an elegant version composed of chicken, mushrooms, peas, noodles, and Madeira sauce—Madame de Lyon's Omelette Brillat Savarin [*sic*]. Anthelme Brillat-Savarin is often remembered only for his many aphorisms:

- Whoever receives friends and does not participate in the preparation of their meal does not deserve to have friends.

- A dessert without cheese is like a beautiful woman with only one eye.

- The discovery of a new dish confers more happiness on humanity than the discovery of a new star.

- Tell me what you eat and I will tell you what you are.

- A man who was fond of wine was offered some grapes at dessert after dinner. "Much obliged," said he, pushing the plate aside, "I am not accustomed to take my wine in pills."

- To receive guests is to take charge of their happiness during the entire time they are under your roof.

- Cooking is one of the oldest arts and one that has rendered us the most important service in civic life.

- The pleasure of the table belongs to all ages, to all conditions, to all countries, and to all areas; it mingles with all other pleasures, and remains at last to console us for their departure.

Brillat-Savarin, however, was also an accomplished philosopher, civic servant, lawyer, and judge, as well as, of course, a celebrated gastronome.

Noted literary gourmand and private detective Nero Wolfe, created by Rex Stout, includes a recipe for a misleadingly titled Plain Omelet in the short novel *And Be a Villain*. A wonderfully unique omelet of mushrooms and almonds makes for lunch in *Plot It Yourself*, and there is a beautiful strawberry dessert omelet in *If Death Ever Slept*. Omelets also appear, sometimes metaphorically, as in "Jeeves Makes an Omelette," in the works of P. G. Wodehouse. In *A Damsel in Distress*, Geoffrey Raymond, lunching with Maud, reminiscences about a perfect French omelet of chicken livers sautéed in butter, at "a small, unpretentious place near the harbour. I shall always remember it."

In *Alexander's Bridge*, Willa Cather describes a "delightful omelette stuffed with mushrooms and truffles." Less sophisticated and decidedly more improvisational is the Omelette à la Samoset, described in Jack London's *The Night-Born* as made of egg powder, tinned mushrooms, and a few other unnamed ingredients. Thomas Pynchon's *Gravity's Rainbow* hints at a banana omelet.

A savory omelet of sage, thyme, mint, parsley, and onion almost makes an ominous appearance in Beatrix Potter's *The Tale of Jemima Puddle-Duck*. Likewise in the category of almost omelets is the chick a hungry Pinocchio releases as he contemplates what to do with an egg he has found not long after Cricket dies at his hand.

Presidential omelets, or rather, imaginary omelets prepared by real presidents, feature in an episode of Garrison Keillor's *Prairie Home Companion* based on the idea—not entirely frivolous—that "You don't know what a president would be like until they cook you eggs." Barack Obama's "Dream Omelet" "gives your life meaning. Eggs. Cheese. Onions. Tomatoes. . . ." Among the first, if not the very first of cookbooks to introduce Americans to the presidential kitchen was *The White House Cook Book: A Comprehensive Cyclopedia of Information for the Home*, published in 1887. Included were 21 recipes for omelets, including two for tomato omelets, said to be a favorite of James Polk. James Madison favored a crab omelet. Herbert Hoover was fond of ham omelets, and First Lady Jacqueline Kennedy was partial to sweet omelets, and especially of an "Omelet Surprise Pompadour," which was not an omelet at all, but rather a dessert molded to resemble an omelet. Richard Nixon favored a Spanish omelet, so-called because it was served with a "Spanish-style" sauce of onions, tomatoes, and julienned green peppers. Gerald Ford was fond of egg foo yong for dinner.

In the category of imaginary omelets might be musician and composer David Amram's "crazy" omelet for the great jazz saxophonist Charlie Parker, composed of fried onions, marmalade, maple syrup, bacon, tomatoes, hot garlic, mayonnaise, and cheese sauce. Amram scored the film *Splendor in the Grass*, and is the composer of well over a hundred other works. Another fanciful omelet (one hopes) might be a "perfect plain omelet," described by the Marquis de Sade, writing in *120 Days of Sodom* (1785), as "served piping hot on the buttocks of a naked woman and 'eaten with an exceedingly sharp fork.'" Omelets appear with some frequency in the works of Edgar Allan Poe as well. In addition to the well-known story "Le Duc de L'Omelette," in which Le Duc dies not of an omelet but of an ortolan, in the short story, "Bon-Bon," Poe describes as "inestimable" a regal "Omelet of the Queen," made of eggs with chicken puree, cream sauce, and vegetables. (I once considered calling my mother the "Queen of Omelets," but I thought better.)

The Artistic Omelet

I mentioned earlier that Salvador Dalí occasionally carried an omelet in his pocket and that he once autographed a Cheddar omelet. Here are

the details: When an overeager fan approached Dalí during lunch, "the eccentric artist whipped out a pink marker and signed his half-finished omelet, much to the dismay of his fan." "Art should be edible," Dalí announced.

Dalí's works of art includes three with omelets in the title:

- *Figure—Omelettes* (1934)

- *Omelette About to Be Irreparably Crushed by Hands* (1934)

- *Omelettes with Dynamic, Mixed Herbs* (1934)

Some of these works are reprinted in Dalí's surrealist cookbook, *Les Diners de Gala*. Sadly, this extraordinary but deeply flawed cookbook includes no omelets. In its stead, you might consider this recipe for "Sicilian Headland," from *The Futurist Cookbook*, a manifesto of the futurist movement published in 1932: "Chop together tuna, apples, olives and little Japanese nuts. Spread the resulting paste on a cold egg and jam omelette."

Dalí's comments about edible art invite us to distinguish between omelets *in* art and omelets *as* art. An omelet can indeed be a work of art, no less an expression of an artist's voice than a watercolor or sculpture.

But even more, an omelet is a canvas upon which to make one's mark. (To make a work of art of your own, see my recipe for a Finger Paint Frittata, page 000.) Picasso is well known for a recipe for an Omelette à l'Espagnole, and Paul Cézanne's recipes include a fine mushroom omelet prepared with mushrooms, leeks, parsley, and garlic—and note, too, that an old housewives' trick of adding a spoonful of vinegar will help. Claude Monet's cooking journals include a recipe for a lovely soufflé omelet with sugar and grated lemon rind.

Eggs are a staple of fine art (think Diego Velázquez, *An Old Woman Cooking Eggs*, or Salvador Dalí, *Oeufs sur le plat*, or Paul Cézanne, *Bread and Eggs*), but omelets as subjects of fine art are less common. An important exception is Andy Warhol's 1959 work *Omelet Greta Garbo*, "always to be eaten alone in a candlelight room." Ironically, Garbo claimed to be unable to make an omelet herself, professing "I can't make an omelette. That's a lot of trouble. You have to stand there and watch it and then you slop it over on one side. I've never done one. I've seen somebody do it. I avoid everything which is work except labor work. That I can do. Hard labor I can do. . . . You mess it up first in a bowl, no? . . . It doesn't have to be a very hot pan? Maybe I'll try it."

The Musical Omelet

A great many classical musicians are immortalized in omelets, among them Bizet (ham, tomatoes, green peppers, onions, rice, and parsley), Chopin (ham, mushrooms, croutons, garlic, cheese), Debussy (ham, eggplant, onions, fines herbes, and tomato sauce), Mozart (ham, artichoke hearts, garlic, parsley, cheese), and Saint-Saëns (chicken, mushrooms, croutons, tarragon, fines herbes).

Somewhat less common are musical compositions that honor the omelet. The most obvious is Mozart's obscure (and still) lost Symphony No. 42, provocatively entitled "Fantasy Frittata Facile."* A poisoned omelet makes a dramatic appearance in a comical one-act opera by

---

* Please do not go looking for this. I made it up.

Georges Bizet entitled *Le Docteur Miracle*: The "Omelette Quartet," as it is known, sets the stage for a miraculous cure by Doctor Miracle (the again-disguised Silvio who, costumed as a domestic servant, had prepared the mortiferous omelet).

How to Eat an Omelet

I love food movies. I even teach a course on food and film at my university, ostensibly because movies about food are also movies about power, scarcity, conflict, family, love and hate, and all sorts of things any self-respecting political scientist ought to study. Mostly, though, I just love food movies, so why not?

One of my favorite food movies is *Big Night*. If you have not seen it, skip to the next paragraph or proceed straight to Netflix. If you have seen it, then you will remember the dramatic closing scene. Not yet reconciled to each other, or to Paradise lost (Paradise is the name of their failing restaurant on the New Jersey coast), Secondo (Stanley Tucci) prepares a simple omelet to share with his brother Primo (Tony Shalhoub). As the omelet cooks on the stove, Secondo reaches for two white plates. When the omelet is ready, Secondo gives part of it to waiter Cristiano (Marc Anthony), along with last night's bread, and takes part of it for himself, leaving some of the egg in the pan. When Primo enters the kitchen, weary and wary, Secondo pulls out another plate. The brothers eat silently, arms on each other's shoulders. The brothers, the bread, and the omelet are more than a metaphor in this scene—their simplicity, their authenticity, their communion, is life itself.

Big Night tells us something about how to eat an omelet. (With good bread. Nothing is more honest than good bread.) It is unusual in doing so. There are hundreds of books and thousands of recipes to tell us how to *make* an omelet, but I have found none that tells us how to *eat* one. We can find instruction elsewhere. The Corinthian injunction "Let us eat" is an invitation to live in the present and to enjoy our company and ourselves. It tells us to *savor* the meal and the experience; "No detail is too small, no book or recipe too long, to be savoured." To *savor* a meal is to take delight in creation, no matter how glorious or common. It is to take delight in the comfort of the familiar or in the surprise of an unexpected taste. "Delight in the act of cooking," the Episcopalian theologian and food writer Robert Farrar Capon observed, "is one of the oldest and nearest things in the world."

To savor has another, no less important meaning. To *savor* is to be mindful, to appreciate what is before us. Voltaire reminds us that "Appreciation is a wonderful thing: It makes what is excellent in others belong to us as well." No less important, it makes us human. Dogs, it is said, "eat to give their bodies rest; man dines and sets his heart in motion." Partly true. My mother's dog, Daisy, taught me that dogs dine no less than people do, and that is what makes them human. "We were given appetites, not to consume the world and forget it, but to taste its goodness and hunger to make it great."

There is also the important question of whether to eat an omelet in the company of others or in the company of ourselves alone. Marilyn Hacker urges us to eat the omelet "with somebody you'll remember." (I suggest your dog.) I suppose that makes Hacker an Epicurean, a disciple of a school of Greek philosophy that believed that who we eat with matters more than what we eat. Contrast this advice with Warhol's *Omelet Greta Garbo*, which is "always to be eaten alone in a candlelight room." I hold with Warhol: Eating alone is as much an act of communion as eating with others.

There is one final part of what it means to savor a meal: One must *taste* it. I had an instructor in culinary school who constantly admonished us to taste the food while we were cooking it. "If you're not tasting," he would say, "you're not cooking." The same is true of eating. Too often, we eat without tasting what we eat. Renowned omelettier Madame Romaine de Lyon observed this in her many years at her famed bistro, concluding, "in America it is common for people to eat several things at once, in hysterical combination, losing the taste of each."

Conclusion: How an Omelet Means

By now, I hope to have persuaded you of the importance of omelets in human affairs. But this book isn't really about omelets—it is about what the search for the perfect omelet has to teach us about how to cook and how to live. *The Perfect Omelet* is a metaphor and a ministry.

This is the place, then, to ask: What does an omelet mean? The better question is a simple one with an unimaginably complex answer: *How* does an omelet mean? I borrow the question from John Ciardi's classic essay on how to read a poem. We cannot understand a poem, Ciardi proposes, simply by reading or memorizing it. A poem can be known only through experience. The question we should ask, he writes, is not *what* a poem means, but *how* it means. "It is the experience, not the Final Examination, that counts . . . : once one has learned to experience the poem as a poem, there inevitably arrives a sense that one is also experiencing himself as a human being."

This is the lesson of our search for the perfect omelet: One cannot get a perfect omelet by reading a recipe or even a book about omelets. An omelet is not of the "school of fixed answers." We cannot know what a recipe means, *how* it means, simply by reading it. The meaning of any recipe resides in the experience of making it. A recipe is not a command—it is an invitation. The way to cook, the title of one of Julia Child's masterpieces, is by cooking. The way to a perfect omelet is to make one. Crack an egg. Pick up a pan. In cooking, mindfully and playfully, we experience ourselves as human beings.

Still you may ask: Why look to *omelets* for the meaning of life? Why not meat loaf, or potpies, or carrots? Supreme Court Justice Oliver Wendell Holmes Jr. has answered this question for us, though he may not have had omelets in mind. (On the other hand, maybe he did. Holmes's father, Oliver Wendell Sr., was something of a sophisticate of the morning meal, having written the best-selling *The Autocrat of the*

Breakfast–Table and two sequels, *The Professor of the Breakfast–Table* and *The Poet at the Breakfast–Table*.)

Here is Justice Holmes in an address to the graduates of Harvard University:

> *All that life offers any man from which to start his thinking or his striving is a fact. And if this universe is one universe, if it is so far thinkable that you can pass in reason from one part of it to another, it does not matter very much what the fact is. For every fact leads to every other by the path of the air. . . . To be master of any branch of knowledge, you must master those which lie next to it; and thus to know anything you must know all.*

Hilaire Belloc was wrong. A person who can make an omelet properly is a person who knows that to know anything you must strive to know everything. All that life offers us is a place from which to start our thinking. If I may paraphrase another book about cooking and philosophy, an omelet is not a bad place to start the journey.

Chapter One:
How to Make a Perfect Omelet

o─┨─◉─┠─o

An egg is always an adventure; the next one may be different.

—OSCAR WILDE

There are several schools of thought about how to make an omelet, each more improbable and complicated than the last. One caucus insists that an omelet must be prepared *this* way and that only a French omelet will do. Another insists that an omelet must be prepared some other way; an authentic omelet, they say, is more frittata than French. Some schools of thought urge us to roll, others to fold, and still others to soufflé. Some writers think omelets have nationalities—there are French omelets, Italian omelets, Spanish omelets, American omelets and, presumably, several others, though these go unremarked.

I hold, however, with Richard Olney. Writing in the classic *Simple French Food* (1983), Olney observed of omelet making, "There are no secrets, no special talent is required, and no method is better than any other." Olney is right, but if no special talent is required, a perfect omelet *does* require three things: the best ingredients, the right pan, and your enthusiastic, unflagging attention.

The Best Ingredients

Good ingredients hide many mistakes.

In wise words often but wrongly attributed to C. S. Lewis, "no clever arrangement of bad eggs ever made a good omelet." No omelet is better than its eggs. Get good, fresh eggs. M. F. K. Fisher tells us that a stale egg is a dishonest egg, and dishonest eggs should be scrambled or, better, discarded. Eggs in your supermarket are typically older than farmers' eggs by a month or more, and unlike wine, eggs do not improve with age. (Eggs do improve, however, with wine.) Supermarket eggs are reliably edible, if undistinguished, and rarely if ever spoiled (if they are, you need to find a better market). But they simply cannot compare to local, organic eggs from a farmers' market. It is difficult to overstate the importance of good eggs.

The best eggs are organic and free-range, but what do these terms mean? Free-range hens are cage-free, but cage-free hens are not necessarily free-range. *Cage-free* means only that the hens are not caged. A cage-free hen may or may not be permitted the run of a barn (there are no rules about how much space the hens should have, except in California), but she is not allowed outside. Free-range

hens usually have access to an outside, protected environment that gives them room to roam . . . if they want to. To make matters even more complicated, free-range eggs are sometimes called "pastured" eggs, but to be very precise, most folks use the term "pastured" to refer to hens that have access to grassed areas and consume a diet comprising mostly plants and insects.

Organic eggs are free of pesticides, fungicides, herbicides, and non-natural fertilizers, but the term *organic* is a source of much confusion and consternation. According to the United States Department of Agriculture (USDA) National Organic Program, *organic* means that the hens are

free-range, free of pesticides, and consume an organic diet. Most definitions would add that the hen must be free of vaccines and antibiotics.

Let's assume you don't raise chickens or live on a farm. (I don't. Yet.) How can you tell if the eggs at your market are honest? You can perform several tests, though some might get you arrested if you try them in the store. To wit:

- *The sink-or-swim test.* Place the egg in a bowl of cold water. (Some authorities salt the water.) Older eggs have more air in them, so . . . an egg that floats is old, and an egg that sinks is fresh. An egg that sinks but stands straight up on its pointy end is iffy. The idea behind this test almost makes sense, but every egg and every eggshell is unique. Some let in more air, some less, irrespective of age. Moreover, the size of the air cell varies from egg to egg. In all, this test is fun (if impractical at the store), but not especially reliable.

- *The shake-and-slosh test.* This method is sometimes called the sound test. The theory, as I understand it, is that an older egg will have thinned and hence will have more room to swim or slosh about if one shakes the egg. Shake the egg next to your ear. If you hear the egg slosh, it's old(er). This test is unreliable for much the same reason that the sink-or-swim test doesn't work. It does, however, have one plain advantage over the sink-or-swim test—this one you might actually be able to try in a grocery store. That is, if your dignity is of no concern.

- *The flame-and-candle test.* Fannie Farmer, one of America's first celebrity chefs and author of the influential *Boston Cooking-School Cook Book*, advised the cook to "Hold in front of candle flame in dark room, and the centre should look clear." The USDA uses a similar high-tech version of the test, called candling, to grade eggs sold commercially.

- *The warm-to-the-cheek test.* This is another method recommended by Farmer: "Place large end to the cheek, and a warmth should be felt." The only warmth I've ever felt is from the flush of embarrassment.

- *Mrs. Beeton's "tongue test."* (*Mrs. Beeton's Book of Household Management*, first published in 1861 and still in print, was profoundly influential.) Beeton advised cooks to "Apply the tongue to the large end of the egg, and if it feels warm, it is new, and may be relied upon as a fresh egg." I am fairly sure this test will get you arrested at most grocery stores, which understandably adhere to the familiar adage "You lick it, you bought it."

- *The color-of-the-egg-white test.* If the white is cloudy, the egg is reasonably fresh. If it is pinkish-white, then the egg has gone or is about to go bad. This test, too, is not much help at the store. You break it, you bought it, seems especially apt for eggs.

There is, happily, one consistently reliable way to determine if your eggs are not fresh. Smell them. If they smell bad, then you may safely surmise that they are not fresh.

A Very Short History of the Egg

Putting aside the question of which came first, doubtless as much of interest to food historians as to anyone else, eggs as an object of human consumption have a history as long-standing as humanity itself. Bird eggs appeared about 150 million years ago, well before the appearance of humanity and of chickens, perhaps confirming the wisdom of Samuel Butler's wry observation that "A hen is only an egg's way of making another egg." Cave drawings of eggs by Cro-Magnons tell us that we have been eating eggs for well over 200,000 years. Most sources trace the development of domesticated hens to south Asia and Southeast Asia before 7500 BC, and Charles Darwin himself thought that modern chickens were the progeny of *Gallus*, or the "Red Jungle Fowl" of Southeast Asia. However, contemporary chickens also owe some of their identity to chickens from southern India.

We know with fair certainty that Egyptians ate eggs of several varieties, including pelican eggs, and we have written accounts of eggs as food from Mesopotamia. As I said in the introduction, the Romans not only consumed eggs (as had the Greeks), they also recorded recipes for eggs that much resemble what we call omelets. Eggs were a staple of European cuisines well before the 1400s, appearing in custards, pastries, beverages, and, as we saw earlier, in omelets.

I do not know of any reliable data concerning how many eggs are produced or consumed worldwide, but in 2015, about 6.66 billion eggs were produced in the United States. The popularity of eggs waxes and wanes, often, it appears, relative to concerns about their healthiness and safety. According to unreleased data from the USDA, Americans on average eat less than one egg per day (roughly 0.68). In 1945, however, at the height of American egg consumption ("peak egg"), the average American consumed over one full egg per day (1.15 to be precise). It might be well to eat more eggs. A recent study conducted by Saint Louis University found that people who ate eggs for breakfast consumed over 300 fewer calories throughout the day than did those who had a bagel.

Egg Anatomy

To appearances, an egg has three parts—a shell, a white (albumen), and a yolk. On closer examination, however, an egg is not just remarkable; it is remarkably complex. The shell is chiefly calcium carbonate (high in vitamin D) and is porous. Unwashed eggs come with a thin coating, sometimes called the bloom, or cuticle, that helps protect them from bacteria. Also helping to protect the egg are the inner and outer membranes, thin, transparent sheaths of protein that envelop the albumen. Every egg also includes an air cell, a small pocket of air that forms at the larger end of the shell between the inner and outer membranes. (Remember that differences in the size of the air cell conspire to make unreliable the sink-or-swim and shake-and-slosh test for freshness.) The thick strand of string that connects the yolk and the white is the chalaza. It helps keep the yolk centered in the shell and is especially prominent in fresher eggs. A very thin membrane, the vitelline membrane, coats just the yolk. If you look very carefully at the yolk, you may see a very small white spot (my father used to call it the egg eye). This spot enables the egg to be fertilized, hence its true name—the germinal disk. The yolk accounts for about a third of an egg's weight and well over half of its protein, vitamins, and minerals.

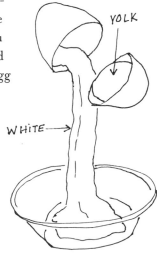

A fresh egg will have a thick albumen and a plump, half-moon yolk. As eggs age, the white thins and the yolk flattens and becomes dull. The yolk of a truly fresh egg is bright, more inclined to orange than the pale yellow of a supermarket egg, and more complex and subtle in taste.

Eggs come in a great variety of colors and shades. The color of an eggshell, you may be surprised to learn, has nothing to do with the hen's diet, but is instead simply a function of the mother's breed. Generally, brownish eggs come from hens with brownish feathers, and whiter eggs from whiter birds. You know, like chocolate milk comes from brown cows. The Araucana chicken lays a bluish-green egg and is the provenance, obviously, of the green eggs in the well-known story by Theodor Geisel.

Although there is no difference in the taste or the color of the egg itself, white eggs are by far more popular in the United States, favored by 88 percent of Americans, whereas 27 percent prefer brown eggs. Your eggs need not be brown to make a perfect omelet, as my mother insisted, but brown eggs do look very nice in a wire basket on the kitchen counter.

Egg Nutrition

Wasn't there once an ad campaign that called eggs "nature's perfect food"? If not, there should be. A single large egg has about 75 calories, is low in fat, a superb source of protein, and has all the nine essential amino acids and a baker's dozen of important vitamins and minerals, including iodine, potassium, and choline. Again, the difference between fresh and store bought eggs is considerable. Fresh eggs have more protein; higher levels of vitamins A, D, and E; more omega-3 fatty acids; and up to one-third less cholesterol. An egg white is a rich source of vitamin B_2 (riboflavin) and of protein, as well as of vitamin B_3 (niacin), magnesium, and potassium. The yolk contains most of an egg's fat and cholesterol, but it is also high in protein and a great many vitamins (A, B_6, B_{12}, D, and K) and minerals (calcium, phosphorous, and iron).

As recently as just a few years ago, however, eggs were the devil's food, whether deviled or not. Eggs were said to be high in cholesterol, saturated fat, and prone to salmonella. Of particular concern was cholesterol. It was widely believed that high levels of blood cholesterol were associated with heart disease. Eggs are relatively high in cholesterol, and hence disfavored by many nutritionists and other medical professionals. Recent research, however, reveals that cholesterol in the diet is not the problem. Indeed, in 2015 the US federal government revised its dietary guidelines concerning cholesterol to remove limits altogether, in favor of concerns about saturated fats, which scientists now think do more to increase blood cholesterol. Egg yolks, low in such fats, are now a recommended source of protein. Moreover, some of the nutrients in eggs are positively correlated with reductions in inflammation associated with heart disease, bone loss, and Alzheimer's disease.

Another long-standing concern about the consumption of eggs has been salmonella. Salmonella is a bacterium that can cause food poisoning. Symptoms of salmonella infection can include diarrhea, abdominal cramps, and fever, and in rare cases may be severe enough to require treatment with antibiotics. Salmonella in eggs has been a particular concern since the 1990s, when scientists discovered a new version, *Salmonella enterica* (SE), present in chickens and in eggs. The Centers for Disease Control (CDC) estimates that about 1 in 10,000 eggs is contaminated, but the risk is higher with eggs that have been factory farmed and are not cage free, free range, or pastured. Undercooked and raw eggs increase the risk, as will leaving raw eggs at room temperature for much longer than an hour or so; "cooking reduces the number of bacteria present in an egg; however, a lightly cooked egg with a runny egg white or yolk still poses a greater risk than a thoroughly cooked egg."

On the Kinds of Eggs

Most of the chicken eggs sold at supermarkets in the United States are graded by the USDA. Eggs may be graded AA, A, and B. AA eggs have a plump yolk and a firm white with an unblemished, unbroken shell. Grade B's, by contrast, have flatter yolks, runnier whites, and a shell that may be stained (this does not affect the safety or the taste of the egg). Most eggs graded B wind up in commercial bakeries. Your market will likely stock only AA and A eggs. You should not assume AA eggs are "better" than A eggs—the grades are assigned when the eggs are packed. All eggs deteriorate in quality as they age, so check the sell-by date on the carton. As noted kitchen scientist Harold McGee writes, "Fresh grade A eggs can be a better buy than old grade AA."

The USDA also grades eggs by size—Jumbo eggs weigh 2.5 ounces each or more (or, McGee notes, about 55 grams) and 30 ounces per dozen. Extra-large eggs are 2.25 ounces per egg and 27 ounces per dozen. Large eggs are 2 ounces each and 24 ounces per dozen. If you look, you may be able to find much smaller eggs. Peewees, for example, are a mere 1.25 ounces each and 15 ounces per dozen, or just half the size of a jumbo. I prefer to use large eggs, simply because they are easy to find, but use what you like, taking care to note that the size of your eggs will affect not only the finished omelet, but also its consistency when the eggs are combined with other ingredients.

In addition to plain white and brown eggs, you may well find several other kinds of eggs at the market. Typically, these are identified as such on the egg carton, which you should read closely.

How to Read an Egg Carton

It might seem unnecessary to tell you how to read an egg carton, but have you ever looked at one? An egg carton is nearly as difficult to decipher as the instructions for your smartphone. In addition to the basic nutritional information required by US federal law, most egg cartons will include information concerning where the eggs were farmed, about how the hens were raised, and sometimes about what they were fed. (An egg is what its mother eats.) Some cartons will include information about salmonella and other food safety issues. Some manufacturers have even begun to include some of this information, concerning omega-3s, for example, or sell-by dates for another, by stamping it on the individual eggs. (Tattooed eggs are an endless source of amusement for young children and occasionally adults, who may think that a hen that can produce an egg with writing on it is a sign. Of something.)

Federal law also requires the carton to indicate the pack-date, or the day on which the eggs were cleaned, graded, and cartoned. The pack date is a three-digit number on the end of the carton, representing the consecutive date of the year. For example, an egg packed on January 1 will be coded as 001 (sometimes called the Julian date or Julian code), on January 31 as 031, and so on. Usually located nearby is the sell-by date. If the eggs were processed in a USDA inspected facility (you'll see the USDA Shield on the carton), the sell-by date cannot exceed the pack date by more than 45 days.

What does the "sell-by" date mean? The sell-by date indicates the date by which the eggs should be sold, not by when they can be safely consumed. If kept in their carton in the fridge, most eggs should be fine for about a month, even if that period extends beyond the sell-by date.

As of January 1, 2015, all eggs sold in California must be certified as CA SEFS Compliant, which stands for California Shell Egg Food Safety Compliant. California law requires eggs in California to come from chickens that have enough room to fully extend their limbs and turn around freely. Even if you do not live in California, you are likely soon to see the CA SEFS shield on the carton. Additionally, most egg cartons will indicate if the eggs are from cage-free, free-range, or pastured hens, and if the eggs are organic, they will indicate that as well. You may also see several other labels. The USDA does not certify most of these labels, but some may be regulated by the state you live in:

Omega-3 eggs come from hens that consume a diet rich in omega-3 fatty acids, including flaxseed, fish oil, and algae. The omega-3 level of eggs is typically about 30 milligrams per egg. Enriched eggs might have as much as 100 to 600 milligrams each.

Pasteurized eggs have been sterilized in a warm water bath (about 130°F). The temperature is hot enough to kill bacteria (including salmonella) but not to cook the egg.

Vegetarian eggs come from hens that consumed no animal products in their feed, which consists chiefly of corn and soy. (Left alone, chickens will eat insects. Vegetarian eggs may indicate that the hens were not free-range or pastured.)

Natural eggs takes the term "natural" to mean that nothing has been added to the eggs—no flavorings, color, brine, or other additives.

No hormones/no antibiotics means neither the hens nor their feed were treated with hormones or antibiotics.

American Humane Certified indicates that the American Humane Association has determined that the hens were raised on farms that meet their standards for the humane treatment of animals. These standards require cage-free barns, prohibit antibiotics and hormones, and prohibit beak trimming.

Animal Welfare Approved indicates the farms on which the hens were raised meet Animal Welfare Approved (AWA) standards, which include access to pastures, a vegetarian diet, and hens that are antibiotic- and hormone-free. The standards also prohibit beak trimming.

On the Care and Maintenance of Eggs

Eggs should be stored in your refrigerator. Eggs age much more quickly at room temperature. Local or farmers' market eggs, unlike the eggs you get from a supermarket, have not been chemically treated, cleaned, or washed. The naturally secreted coating (the bloom, or cuticle) on an unwashed egg helps protect it from bacteria and, almost as important, from the smells of other things in your fridge. Once that coating is removed, an egg is best sheltered in a cold and (reasonably) sterile fridge, and may be kept fresh for about three weeks. Commercial eggs, in contrast, are washed and then coated with a tasteless and odorless mineral oil treatment. Washed or unwashed, keep the eggs in their carton. The carton helps shield the eggs from fluctuations in temperature, which may breed pathogens.

If you don't have a refrigerator (really?), then there are several other ways you can store eggs. I cannot vouch for all of them.

- "The ancient Chinese stored eggs for several years by immersing them in salt and wet clay; cooked rice, salt, and lime; or salt and wood ashes mixed with a tea infusion."

- Fannie Farmer recommended storing fresh eggs in sawdust, pointy end down, or in lime-water, which "may be bought from any druggist's or easily prepared at home," or, from "July to September," in cartons in "cold storage."

- Some folks suggest storing eggs in ground oats, or rice, or salt.

- In the classic cookbook *Good Maine Food*, Marjorie Mosser and Kenneth Roberts advise boiling the eggs for ten seconds and then storing them in an ice chest.

- In a 1933 copy of *the Better Homes Recipe Book*, Marjorie Mills recommended storing eggs in a cooled solution of water glass (a mixture of sodium silicate, the generic name for sodium metasilicate), and boiled water in a cool place.

- Another way to preserve eggs, called "oiling," treats the shell with a very light coating of liquid paraffin or lard.

As eggs age, the amount of air in the shell will increase and the amount of moisture will decline as it is lost through the porous shell. For this reason, it is best to store eggs as Fannie Farmer advised—with the pointy end down. This way, the yolk can float to the top of the egg, where it will have more room to do whatever it is that yolks do.

How to Crack an Egg

No one ever asks, how do I "open" an egg? Instinctively, we know that we must crack it open. But cracking an egg is more complicated than it may seem.

In his classic book *La Technique*, Jacques Pépin suggests that you crack an egg on a flat surface instead of a sharp edge, "which tends to push some of the shell inside the egg, thus introducing bacteria." That makes a lot of sense. Anyone who has ever cracked an egg has gotten a small part of the shell in the bowl. There is an easy way to retrieve it. Use the largest remaining piece of the cracked shell to remove it from the yolk.

With sufficient force, an egg cracks easily, sometimes too easily, but the shell is also exceptionally strong. As Diane Toops has observed, "you cannot break an egg by cupping it in the palm of your hand and squeezing [because] the curved shape of the shell distributes pressure evenly over the shell rather than concentrating it at any one point." With a little practice, however, you can easily master cracking an egg and disposing of the shell with just one hand. If there is any practical purpose for doing so, I have yet to find it. There is, however, a world record you might pursue: The current record for cracking the most number of eggs in an hour with a single hand is 2,318 eggs (an additional 248 eggs were disqualified), held by Bob Blumer, host of a well-known television show called *Glutton for Punishment*.

Other Eggs

We left the matter unresolved in the introduction, but I am firmly of the view that a proper omelet requires eggs. But it doesn't require *chicken* eggs. Humans have eaten eggs from many different creatures for thousands of years, and likely making omelets from them nearly as long.

All the recipes in this book, however, assume you are using chicken eggs. With suitable adjustments, you can make an omelet out of quail eggs (very small, so you'll need more of them, but exceptionally delicious), duck eggs (bigger than a chicken egg, with very large yolks and often with light blue shells), turkey eggs (not much larger than a chicken egg, but with wonderfully speckled shells), goose eggs (not golden), emu eggs (very large—a single emu egg is equivalent to about 14 chicken eggs), and ostrich eggs (the largest and most difficult to find, and almost as difficult to crack; you may need a hammer).

On Butter and Oils

At the market, pick up fresh, unsalted butter. Why unsalted? I prefer unsalted butter because it allows me to control precisely how much salt goes into my food, and because, having used only unsalted butter for many years, I prefer the taste. At least, I imagine that I do. Michael Ruhlman, who admits to a preference for salted butter, nonetheless has concluded that they "yield pretty much the same results." Salted or not, I do feel strongly that you ought to use butter and not a substitute ("Any man who cannot tell the difference between butter and margarine has calluses on the inside of his mouth") and that you should choose your butter wisely.

In the United States, most commercial butters are produced from pasteurized sweet cream and contain at least 80 percent butterfat (most American butters contain slightly more than that, averaging around 81 percent butterfat), whereas "European butters," sometimes sold as cultured butter, typically have a butterfat content of up to 85 percent and often are cultured, like yogurts. As with eggs, the US government grades butter for flavor, body, color, and salt content, ranging from Grade AA (superior quality) to Grade B (standard quality). Most of what you will find in the market is Grade AA. Please 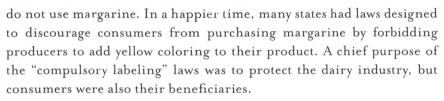 do not use margarine. In a happier time, many states had laws designed to discourage consumers from purchasing margarine by forbidding producers to add yellow coloring to their product. A chief purpose of the "compulsory labeling" laws was to protect the dairy industry, but consumers were also their beneficiaries.

A good butter is more than just an aid to the pan; it contributes a delicate and unique taste to the finished omelet because it has its own delicate and unique taste. Taste several different butters—there *are* differences. A perfect plain omelet requires nothing more than butter and eggs, and the best eggs and the best butter will make a noticeable difference in taste. Some authorities suggest using a clarified butter, or a butter that has had the milk solids and water separated from the butterfat (usually over a very low flame) and removed. Clarified butter has a higher smoke or burning point. (You can achieve a similar effect by combining butter and olive oil.) Unclarified butter will indeed smoke if too hot, but because the eggs are just visiting instead of taking up residence in the pan, I don't find burning to be a worry worth worrying about with omelets.

Many cooks confuse clarified butter with ghee, commonly used in Indian and in many south Asian cuisines, but there can be differences in how they are made, and often differences in flavor. The differences in taste matter, at least for omelets. Ghees are often infused with spices, such as turmeric or cardamom. A flavor-infused ghee is a wonderful *aide d'omelette*, adding complexity and depth. I especially like ghees infused with cumin.

If you have a very fine nonstick pan you might be tempted to use a cooking spray, but I urge you not to do so. Not because the eggs will not stick without help—they might—but because you do not need a lot of oil or butter to prevent an omelet from being stubborn. Just a trace a butter or oil will overcome its resolve and enhance the taste dramatically. With time, some of the more common ingredients in these sprays, such as soy lecithin, may actually make the pan gluey—not good for the pan or for omelets.

For many omelets, especially luncheon and dinner omelets, you might substitute olive oil for the butter. A light olive oil is better suited to and enhances the flavor of many savory omelets. Use the best olive oil you can find (but some very fine olive oils really should not be used for cooking at all, due to their smoke points). I recommend one of the lighter oils, without a pronounced or complicated flavor. If you do use olive oil rather than butter, then consider using an oil from Italy for your frittatas and from Spain for your tortillas. I am *not* suggesting that using a Spanish olive oil makes your tortilla authentic, but there is an element of cultural respect implicit in choosing one's ingredients. This sort of respect is a crucial component

of all good cooking. In addition, there can be very delicate differences in taste.

The same injunction holds when using herbs and other ingredients: Use the best, and fresh is best. Dried herbs may make an Omelette aux herbes, but they cannot make an Omelette aux fines herbes. (Yes, I know that is not what the phrase *aux fines herbes* really means!) Eggs and herbs are comfortable companions. Please do not hesitate to try unusual or uncommon herbs, but do be careful. Some, such as tansy (a common herb in omelets during the Middle Ages), can be toxic in excess.

If you add wine to the eggs (please do), then use the wine you drink and do not be afraid to experiment. Wines also provide the foundation for many superb sauces for omelets, enhancing both the taste and the appearance of the dish. Most omelets prefer a white wine, but why not try a fruity red? Just a tablespoon will blush the omelet. Red wine is not nearly as averse to eggs as you might think. The classic dish Oeufs en meurette, for example, is essentially a recipe for eggs poached in a luscious red wine sauce, typically a Burgundy and often a Beaujolais nouveau. I urge you to try it, even though, as David Rosengarten has observed, "to most Americans this whole idea of poaching an egg in red wine and then serving it with a red wine sauce just doesn't sit right."

In place of water or wine in the mixed eggs, try a tablespoon of miso or shoyu, or maybe yogurt, sour cream, or crème fraîche. Flavored vinegars, "an old housewives' trick," as Paul Cézanne noted, also pair wonderfully with omelets. Vinegars are very much underappreciated in many kitchens. They come in an extraordinary array of tastes and flavors, some common (such as raspberry, or cider, or balsamic) and some unusual (such as coconut or pineapple). I am fond of Champagne vinegars, but use a tablespoon of what you like.

If, having secured the best and freshest ingredients, your omelet still disappoints, then at least you will know who, or rather what, to blame. Blame the pan.

The Right Pan

A practiced cook can make a fine omelet in almost any kind of pan. Well, maybe not my mother's pretty little yellow pan. No good omelet was ever going to roll out of *that* pan. At 6 inches in diameter and impossibly vertiginous, it was best suited for hanging on a wall.

I am sure my mother must have known better. Tucked inside her tattered *Better Homes Recipe Book*, by Marjorie Mills, I found a pamphlet extolling the virtues of the Farberware omelet pan, "the perfect pan for

the perfect omelet." I never saw that pan in my mother's kitchen. She might have kept it hidden (Bravo, Mom!), but I suspect she slipped the flier in the book to remind her of what to ask for next Christmas.

Some say the ability to make an omelet on command is one of the hallmarks of a "true" chef, as Franey's story about making omelets while he was an apprentice illustrates. (Escoffier used a similar test.) Nevertheless, a large part of the aura and mystique of the omelet consists of having not just *any* pan, but the *right* pan. In the words of renowned chef-instructor Anne Willan, "The key to the perfect omelet is the perfect pan." Another prominent chef, Dione Lucas, tells us we "must have a pan you use only for omelets." Why? Part of the reason has historically to do with the elaborate and overly complicated process of seasoning the pan, but this explanation neglects another, more important reason grounded less in practicality than in philosophy. A pan promised only to omelets is a pan uncorrupted and undiverted from its true purpose in life. A pan's singularity of purpose underscores the dignity and the weight, the *gravitas*, of omeletry. In keeping the pan to omelets, we elevate the pan and the omelet; we lend them what each of us deserves even more than love or affection: respect and regard.

Ezra Pound wrote that there is philosophy in an egg. There is a philosophy in a pan as well. Actually, a pan *is* a philosophy. Borrowing from the well-known philosopher Isaiah Berlin, some pans are hedgehogs (they know one thing very well), and some pans are foxes (they know a little about many things). Some pans are gimmicky, some pans are celebrity pans; some pans are cheap, some are expensive. Some pans try to take the hazard out of cooking; others make it more complicated than it has to be. Some pans embrace a philosophy of functionalism or utilitarianism, where we judge the pan solely by its ability to do what it means to do, or of aestheticism, where we measure the pan by its beauty or appearance. A good pan, however, starts with a philosophy of symmetry, a philosophy in which purpose, form, and appearance are in fine balance. A good pan also teaches us about the ethics of caring and respect. We learn this philosophical truth only by *using* and caring for the pan. No measure of reading about the pan, or how to use it, will suffice.

A Perfect Pan, or On the Care and Management of Omelet Pans

Philosophy teaches us that the perfect pan is a hedgehog, not a fox. It must be closely guarded and lovingly attended to, resolute to the single-minded pursuit of the perfect omelet. But what makes the *pan* perfect? Are you surprised to learn that there is much disagreement about this important topic? The venerable *Joy of Cooking*, by Irma S. Rombauer and Marion Rombauer Becker, observes, "Omelette pans generate more tempests than teapots."

A traditional (French) omelet pan is black carbon steel, with a diameter of 7 or 8 inches, and equipped with a long handle. Its care and management are matters of extreme importance and consequence. Because it does not have a nonstick finish, this pan must be seasoned, or "cured." There is no end of instruction about how to season a pan, but the basic process is straightforward: Coat your pan with a sheen of oil and let it rest on a warm burner. Swirl the oil to coat the pan and when the oil is hot, remove the pan from the heat. Let the pan sit, preferably overnight, and then warm the oil again, let it cool, and wipe the excess with a clean towel. A seasoned pan should be cleaned only with salt and a dry towel. Soap and water remove the finish and so must be avoided. This is another reason that your pan should be kept to omelets.

It may seem silly, but the elaborate ritual of seasoning and salting has both practical and spiritual meaning. An improperly seasoned pan will not release the finished omelet onto the plate. Just as significantly, a neglected pan is a tangible sign of the cook's lassitude. No good can come from such a pan, but it is the fault of the cook, not of the pan.

For those of us not trained at Le Cordon Bleu or the Culinary Institute of America (and even for those who were!), a perfect pan is 8 or 9 inches in diameter, just the right size for a two- or three-egg omelet. It should be nonstick and possessed of an ovenproof handle. Look for a substantial pan with gently sloping or entirely rounded sides. Think of the shape of an egg: There is no seam, no mark, to delineate the bottom or the top of the egg from its sides. Similar for the pan: There ought not to be a seam or a crease that distinguishes the sides of the pan from the bottom. This softly rounded shape encourages the eggs to take the form of an omelet, making it easier to roll both in and out of the pan and onto the plate. The heavy weight of the pan helps conduct heat evenly. Oddly, such a pan can be difficult to find. Even pans sold unambiguously as "omelet pans" by boutique stores or celebrity chefs often have sides and slopes that are unsuitably steep, or handles that disqualify them from the oven. Some of them are very fine pans indeed, but in my judgment, they are flawed. My judgment matters, as does yours, because a pan is personal.

These Are a Few of My Favorite Pans . . .

I have near about to ten pans I use for omelets, including my mother's pan and some very expensive and fancy ones. However, you do not need to purchase something very expensive or even very attractive to make a fine omelet. Two of my favorite (by "favorite," I mean no one else can use them) are no-name, inexpensive pans that I picked up at discount stores. One I have had so long that I can no longer make out the manufacturer. It has a metal handle, is nonstick stainless steel, is about 9 inches, and is perfectly rolled on the sides—there is no seam to mark where the sides depart the bottom. It is heavy. It feels solid. It conducts heat beautifully.

The other skillet I picked up at Marden's (a discount store) in Maine just a year or two ago. It is Chinese, I think, with a cream-colored non-stick ceramic coating. It, too, has perfectly rounded sides, and because the pan is cast iron, it is especially well suited for small frittatas and soufflé omelets finished in the oven.

My newest favoritest pan, however, is not a Chevy or a Ford. It's a sleek, sporty Maserati. Except it is not Italian, it is Japanese, manufactured by a company called Iwachu. I said earlier that a good pan is a combination of function and form. This pan is the embodiment of the philosophy

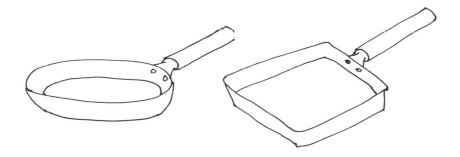

of symmetry: It is a single, sculpted piece of heavy cast iron, has gently sloping sides, and is ovenproof. No less important, it is pleasing to the eye, and the slope farthest from the handle (itself a work of art) is slightly elevated. This unique configuration helps the eggs take the traditional shape of an omelet when it rolls onto the plate.

Possessed now of a perfect pan, you may find it helpful to acquire one or two additional implements, though they are not strictly necessary. A high-quality, heat-resistant spatula will help keep the eggs moving in the pan and to dispatch them from the pan to plate. I prefer a somewhat floppy spatula to a stiffer one, with an old-fashioned wooden handle, but silicone spatulas hold up to the heat better. A little research will turn up several specialized spatulas, just for omelets.

These are unnecessary if not insulting, designed chiefly to play upon our fear of failure ("We found that, in order to make the perfect omelet, a turner needs a combination of both flexible and sturdy materials. Thus, the Flip & Fold Omelet Turner was born"). I would not forbid you from using a flip-and-fold spatula, but I will be disappointed if you do. By the way, you do not need a special whisk, either (though I am sure you can find one, said to be just for omelets). A fork will do just fine.

An Enthusiastic Hand

With superior ingredients and a pan ample to the task, there is just one more essential element for making the perfect omelet: your uncompromised attention. This is a crucial part of the philosophy of the perfect omelet. The good things in our world require our unweaning attention, the full measure of our love and affection. Good things, omelets among them, must be (at)tended to. As one of my teachers, the noted political philosopher Sheldon Wolin, once wrote: "[Tending] implies active care of things close at hand, not mere solicitude . . . the crucial point is that tendment is tempered by the feeling of concern." To *tend*, both colloquially and in the particular sense Wolin describes, is to care for, to show solicitude and concern about and for that to which we tend. In tending to omelets, we nourish ourselves.

To tend means also to pay *attention*. Attention is "concentration on the present moment." Attention to the minuscule moment is what opens us to the possibility of seeing beyond ourselves "by making us attentive to the infinite value of each instant." Attention is "a constant vigilance of the spirit."

The vigilance of our spirit is not too much to ask when we omelet. Even the most complicated of omelets requires no more than a few minutes to cook. Once you have begun an omelet you cannot abandon it, not even for a moment, because "an omelet is one of the things that cannot wait." Neglecting an omelet in the pan does not always portend an inferior result, but it reflects poorly on the omelet and on the pan, and unfairly so. This time it is not the pan but you at fault. No matter. Try again. No philosophy of life or of cooking asks for more.

How to Plate an Omelet

The first rule of plating is the most important rule: Hot foods should be served on warm plates, cold foods on cold plates. The rule applies with no exception for omelets; indeed, it applies with greater urgency.

Omelets are tender and delicate—like a startled paramour, a warm omelet is likely to shy into itself if surprised by a cold touch.

We discussed earlier how seeing is tasting. What makes something taste good is not simply a claim about how something sits on the tongue—it is also about what *looks* appetizing. Make your omelet look nice on the plate. The fine art of garnishing is about making a dish satisfying to all our senses. Garnishing an omelet begins with a slight sheen of butter and dressing it with complementary colors, such as mint green and strawberry red. If you want to, you can purchase all sorts of fancy and complicated kitchen tools just for garnishing, but they aren't necessary. All you need is a sharp paring knife with which to fan a fruit or, failing that, a sprig of basil or parsley.

On the Types of Omelets & Four Master Recipes

There are as many kinds of omelets as there are fish in the sea. (I was going to say, as there are sorts of snowflakes, but the fish in the sea metaphor, if just as tired, gets me to thinking appetizing thoughts about seafood omelets. Yum.) Like people, omelets take a variety of shapes and forms. They may be rolled, folded, flipped, or flat. They may be flavored or filled, flambéed, or sauced; they may be savory or sweet. They can be served as an appetizer, an entrée, or a dessert.

Omelets can be as homey as hash or as refined as truffles. Unembellished, for example, an Omelette nature is the purest of comfort foods. In this, its most elemental form, an omelet is simply eggs, butter, salt, and pepper. Gild this humble omelet with lobster, shrimp, and truffles, and sauce it with fresh tomatoes and a dash of cream and butter, and it is now an Omelette dieppoise, perhaps the single most iconic representation of French haute cuisine.

Here I present four master recipes, one for each of the main varieties of omelets: French, or rolled; American, or folded; Flat; and Soufflé. My taxonomy of omelets is ordained not by history, tradition, science, religion, or gastronomy, but rather by a philosophy of how to cook. I have chosen them because each involves a different technique for making a nearly innumerable variety of omelets. Techniques are the grammar of recipes. In fact, techniques are more important than recipes. "If you know a single technique," Michael Ruhlman observes, "you immediately have hundreds of recipes at hand." Mastering each of the four techniques for omelet making that I describe here opens up a nearly limitless number of possibilities for finding your own perfect omelet.

For that reason, too, the formatting and presentation of the four master recipes is a bit uncommon. The headnotes run a little long, and sometimes they describe different techniques and alternatives. My excuse is that the four master recipes are not really recipes at all—at least, not in any conventional sense. They are meant to teach, to raise points to think about. Think of them not as recipes, much less as commands or prescriptions from the school of fixed answers, but as invitations to play. Play, Plato reminds us, is serious because it is fun.

The Classic French (Rolled) Omelet

Omelette nature

This is a simple omelet and the most difficult to master. Its success depends on good, fresh ingredients and a confident hand. With all the ingredients ready, and a hot pan, it should take no more than a minute or two to prepare. Escoffier composed his omelet with three eggs, but he was Escoffier; I find two eggs a little easier to roll in the skillet (especially in an 8-inch pan). If you prefer three eggs, or just want to channel your inner Escoffier, then try it.

The classic omelet may or may not include 1 tablespoon of water. Some of us think it makes the omelet a little fluffier. (There is a good reason for thinking this: As the water vaporizes during the cooking process it creates small bubbles in the eggs, thus making them fluffier.) Others insist that it dilutes the flavor of the eggs. I am agnostic, but I do believe that pretty much anything that uses water is improved if you replace it with wine. This is certainly true of omelets, especially luncheon and dinner omelets. Do not add milk! Milk seems to toughen the eggs. For sentimental reasons, I prefer to add a drop or two of Tabasco. And brown eggs.

If you burn the butter, you must clean out the pan and start over; nothing worthwhile can be done with burnt butter. If it has simply browned, however, do not give up. Lower the heat and continue with your omelet as though nothing untoward has happened. Add a few drops of vinegar and a small sliver of butter to make a sauce. Cook the sauce until the butter is coffee brown, and serve it as an Omelette beurre noisette in homage to Escoffier's famous recipe for Oeufs au beurre noir. Perfect!

....

SERVES 1

2 eggs, mixed
1 tablespoon water
2 or 3 drops Tabasco
Salt and freshly ground black pepper
1 tablespoon unsalted butter or olive oil, plus a pat of butter for garnish
Parsley, chervil, or chives for garnish

Preheat a nonstick, 8- or 9-inch skillet over medium to medium-high heat.

Whisk the eggs, water, Tabasco, salt, and pepper with a fork until just combined. Do not overmix the eggs. Stop when the eggs just begin to foam, about 15 to 20 seconds; there is no need to beat them into submission. Too much air may cause the omelet to be dry and arid. On the other hand, in some recipes we will want to beat the eggs for a very long time indeed. As Narcissa Chamberlain has observed, "eggs seem to go through three stages in the beating. [Too long] tends to take all the joy out of them. . . . A much longer beating brings them around again to the frothy stage and produces a fine creamy omelette." I don't know where Chamberlain learned this, but I learned it by watching the cooks at one of America's culinary shrines, the Waffle House, where they mix the eggs in an old-fashioned milk shake mixer. And no, I'm not kidding. Some of the best omelets I have ever had were at the Waffle House.

Melt the butter in the skillet, swirl to coat the pan, and when the butter bubbles and sizzles but is not smoking or brown, pour the eggs into the pan. The correct heat is a crucial element in omeletry. Too hot and the eggs color too quickly; not hot enough and the eggs do not congeal properly. At just the right heat, an omelet almost cooks itself. There are several ways to know whether the heat is correct. If the butter bubbles, the temperature is textbook. If it has browned or burned, however, then the heat is too high. Alternatively, hold your hand a few inches over the pan. At medium heat, most of us can do so comfortably till about the count of five.

Pour the eggs into the pan and let them sit undisturbed for about 5 seconds. With a fork or a spatula, move the eggs in a circular pattern, from the outside of the pan to the inside. At the same time, using sharp, short, and controlled motions, keep the skillet moving back and forth. Moving both the eggs and the pan helps create soft, small curds that give a rolled omelet texture and taste.

After the eggs have begun to form curds, but before they stiffen completely, perhaps 10 seconds, remove the pan from the heat and use the fork to "roll" the eggs from the far side of the pan to the side closest to you. Do not let the eggs brown or stiffen; the perfect French omelet has a soft, creamy center (the French describe it as *baveuse*), and little to no color (browning). *The White House Cookbook* (1901), written by Hugo Ziemann, a chef for Prince Napoleon (son of Napoleon III) and several prominent restaurants, including the Hotel Splendide in Paris and the Hotel Richelieu in Chicago, wrote that when done, the omelet "will be firm around the edge, but creamy and light inside."

Now you must convince the omelet onto a warm plate. Grab underneath the handle of the pan with the palm of your hand, thumb on top of the handle, and tilt the pan toward the plate. Your omelet should slide easily toward the bottom of the pan. Every omelet wants to be plated, but some are a little shy and a few, but only a few, are simply stubborn. If your omelet resists, give it a gentle shove with your spatula.

Invert the omelet, seam side down, onto the plate. The plated omelet ought to resemble the back of your hand, slightly rounded and slightly elevated. A higgledy-piggledy omelet may be tidied up by using a clean hand towel or a spatula to entice it gently into the proper posture.

Dress the omelet with a thin pat of butter (a small piece of butter on the top will make the omelet glisten). A green garnish of parsley, chervil, or chives is a nice touch as well.

....

Variation: For a nice luncheon or dinner omelet, replace the water with white wine; a grassy sauvignon blanc is a good choice, but use what you drink. Instead of butter, use a tablespoon of a good olive oil. Served with a green salad, crusty bread, and more wine, a spirited Omelette nature makes a fine supper.

....

> **A TIP FROM MY MOTHER:** Use only fresh brown eggs brought to room temperature.

The American Diner (Folded) Omelet

This recipe for a cheese omelet is a greasy spoon standard and more than worthy of its patrician French cousin. Happily, you can find this omelet in any diner in any town. This omelet, delicious though it is, is not the classic and equally delectable Omelette américaine, which includes diced tomatoes sautéed lightly in butter and diced bacon.

Unlike a French omelet, in which both the pan and the eggs are agitated, this omelet sits quietly in the pan and, when it is done, is folded in half to resemble a half-moon. Many cooks find it easier to make than the classic French omelet. The result is a firmer, browner, and less runny omelet that may seem more familiar to what Americans call an omelet. There are endless variations, some of which I suggest throughout this book.

....

Serves 1

2 eggs, mixed
1 tablespoon water
2 or 3 drops Tabasco
Salt and freshly ground black pepper
1 tablespoon unsalted butter
2 tablespoons grated or shredded cheese
Cheese triangle for garnish
Melon slice or fanned strawberry for garnish

Preheat a nonstick, 8- or 9-inch skillet over medium to medium-high heat.

Whisk the eggs, water, Tabasco, salt, and pepper with a fork until just combined—do not overmix them.

Melt the butter in the skillet, swirl to coat the pan, and when the butter sizzles, add the eggs. Swirl the eggs so they cover the entire bottom of the pan. Let the eggs sit quietly for about 10 seconds.

recipe continues . . .

Holding the handle of the pan and using a spatula, pull the uncooked egg toward the center of the pan, proceeding calmly and deliberately around the compass, north to south to east to west. Use a spatula to lift the eggs from the rim of the pan, and move the remaining uncooked egg under the cooked portion.

When the eggs have set, add the cheese to the center of the omelet. It is important not to use too much cheese, or to incorporate it before the eggs have begun to set—too much cheese, too soon, may cause the omelet to stick.

Using a spatula, fold the omelet in half, moving from the outside of the pan to the inside. You may find it helpful to tilt the pan just a little bit.

Turn out the omelet onto a warm plate. Garnish by placing a triangle of cheese on top of the omelet along with a slice of melon or a fanned strawberry, and serve immediately. The whole process should not take more than a couple of minutes.

> **A TIP FROM MY MOTHER:** A fanned fruit, such as a strawberry, makes a lovely garnish. With a sharp paring knife, slice the strawberry thinly, about the width of a dime, from just below the green leaves to the pointy end. Take care not to slice all the way through the plump end of the strawberry or through the green leaves—we want the chubby end to remain intact. Gently spread (my mother would say "divaricate") the sliced berry into the shape of a handheld fan.

Flat Omelets: Frittatas & Tortillas

Frittata with Two Summer Squashes

Frittatas are just like French omelets, only different, and, for most folks, easier to make. They may be served hot, warm, or at room temperature. If a French Omelet is the serious, eldest child, a frittata is the baby in the family, fun and playful. In the words of Michelle Maisto, "Frittatas . . . require only eggs and imagination."

A frittata differs from the familiar omelet in three ways. First, and most important, frittatas are flat—there is nothing to roll or fold. Second, we cook the fillings first and place them directly into the egg mixture, instead of gift-wrapping them between a top and bottom blanket of eggs. I prefer to cook (and season) the fillings in the same pan. Finally, whereas most omelets are decidedly sedentary and must be persuaded to the plate, a frittata can be acrobatic, if the cook is sufficiently adventuresome!

Frittatas make an admirable lunch or dinner for four persons or more, in part because they are easy to prepare and elegant to serve, but I especially like to make individual frittatas for one or two persons—they are quick to prepare, forgiving, and present beautifully on the plate. The following recipe serves four, and should be cooked in a 10- or 12-inch nonstick, ovenproof skillet. A frittata and a salad dressed lightly with oil make an excellent brunch or dinner, as I first learned at a small dinner party hosted very late one night by a staffer at the American Embassy in Santiago.

The most obvious and most important variation to a frittata is a Tortilla española (potato-onion tortilla), although one might maintain as easily that it is the tortilla that is standard and the frittata the variation. Nations go to war over less (think of the Pastry War between France and Mexico in 1838). Like a frittata, a tortilla may be served hot, warm, or at room temperature. Sliced into wedges or small squares and served as a small tapa, or finger food, they are a staple at tapas bars. A full tortilla makes a fine late night supper.

One should never use milk in a traditional omelet, but for some reason I do not fully understand (likely to do with the fat, which discourages egg proteins from pairing, making the curds more tender), milk or a similar dairy (yogurt or ricotta, perhaps, or even crème fraîche) pairs well with frittatas. I use a quarter-cup of dairy for every six eggs.

⅓ cup sliced yellow summer squash
⅓ cup sliced zucchini
Salt and freshly ground black pepper
1 tablespoon olive oil, plus 1 additional tablespoon (optional)
6 eggs, mixed
2 tablespoons water or white wine
Basil, parsley, mint, or lavender sprig for garnish (optional)
Nasturtiums or squash blossoms for garnish (optional)

Preheat the broiler.

Preheat a nonstick, ovenproof 10- or 12-inch skillet (a seasoned cast-iron skillet is also a good choice) over medium to medium-low heat.

Lightly sauté the squash with salt and pepper in 1 tablespoon of olive oil. The squash are finished cooking when they have softened. Do not brown the squash—we want them to retain their color and shape.

Whisk the eggs, water, salt, and pepper with a fork until just combined—do not overmix.

Heat an additional tablespoon of olive oil, if necessary, swirl to coat the pan, and when it shimmers, add the eggs to the squash. Cook over low heat until the eggs set, approximately 5 to 6 minutes. If there is uncooked egg, lift an edge up and tilt the pan so the uncooked egg runs underneath the cooked egg.

The easiest way to finish a frittata is to place it under the broiler until the eggs finish cooking and are slightly browned; this should take no more than a minute or two. I use this method when I want to layer the top of the frittata with grated cheese. Take care not overcook the frittata—the center is essentially a custard. It should be firm but still creamy, like a cheesecake or a pudding.

Once the frittata has cooked it must be plated and garnished. To plate it, carefully lift the edges of the frittata with a spatula and give it a slight shake in the pan to confirm that the frittata is willing to move. Then slide the frittata onto a plate. (If you have cooked your frittata in an attractive cast-iron pan, I might leave it there.) One very pretty and easy way to garnish a frittata is to place a sprig of basil or parsley, or perhaps mint, in the very center of the plated dish. My favorite garnish is a sprig of lavender, which is not only edible but also adds brilliant color. Nasturtiums or squash blossoms (especially for a Frittata with Two Summer Squashes!) are a nice touch as well.

Finishing a Frittata

There are several ways to finish a frittata. Two of them, including the broiler method described in this recipe, are very easy and reliable. Two others promise an element of adventure.

The Oven: Another method for making a frittata takes somewhat longer, but it is nearly foolproof. Preheat the oven to 350°F. Start the frittata in a warm, ovenproof pan on the stove over medium-low heat. Cooking the frittata too fast will make it dry.

After the edges of the egg begin to set, about 5 minutes, loosen them gently with a spatula, and then put the pan into the oven for approximately 10 to 12 minutes. (How long you should cook the frittata will depend on how many eggs you use and the size of your pan.) The frittata is complete when the eggs have puffed and the top is slightly springy to the touch, like a cheesecake. The result is very much like a soufflé.

The Inversion: A third method for finishing a frittata (and the traditional way of finishing a tortilla) is to cook it on the stove until the top of the eggs are set, occasionally moving the uncooked egg under the cooked edges (how long will depend on how many eggs you use and the size of your pan). Invert the frittata onto a dinner plate, and then return it to the pan over medium-low heat to finish cooking. This last step in the pan should take only a minute or two. The inverted top should be golden brown. The inversion method seems to be the most common prescription, but I find that it causes many beginners more anxiety than is necessary.

The Flip: If it is anxiety you want, then the best (and funniest?) way to finish a frittata is to flip it. Admittedly, flipping a frittata takes a bit of practice, and works only with small ones, but it is not that hard to do, and the show-off factor is undeniable. As with a rolled omelet, the trick is to let the omelet know who is in charge. Fear and frittatas do not mix. Approach the task confidently and without apprehension.

To flip a frittata: First, loosen the edges of the frittata with a spatula, and swirling the pan like a glass of wine (and keep a glass nearby; it greatly increases one's confidence), confirm that the eggs are amenable to moving and not stuck to the pan. Then, with a sharp, backward motion, confident and controlled, pull the pan toward your body. The motion should set the eggs moving away from you and into the air. Now, keeping your eye on the egg, center the pan so the eggs return home. Most beginners greatly overestimate how high the eggs should be in the air. It is much easier to return the frittata to the pan if you do not aim for the ceiling. Richard  Olney has observed that "the apprehensive novice often fails to produce more than a stubborn shudder from the omelet—or it may take flight." A flying frittata makes a poor meal for one's self or for guests, but it is a very fine snack for the dog, as generations of dogs in my family (and Willie, my bichipoo) can attest.

As I said, a little practice helps a lot. If you don't have a dog, an inexpensive and easy way to practice a flip is to purchase a small bag of dried beans. Place the beans in a cold pan, and flip away. This is much easier if you keep the beans *in* the bag.

Do not be afraid to flip and fail. The philosophy behind the perfect omelet urges us to try, and many (by many, I mean me) have flipped and failed before you. You are certain to fail at much more important things in life; failing to flip a frittata isn't like doing poorly on an exam or forgetting to feed the fish. No less a dignitary than Napoleon himself was miserable at omelet making, once exclaiming, "I have given myself credit for more exalted talents than I possess." On the other hand, tightrope walker Charles Blondin, famous for crossing Niagara Falls in 1859, was known to prepare an omelet while on the wire.

Soufflé and Spirited Omelets

Soufflé Omelette aux fines herbes

The classic soufflé omelet was the life's work of Mère Annette Poulard, propri-etor of an inn outside Mont Saint-Michel in the 1870s. She cooked her renowned omelets in a very long-handled pan in a fireplace. Her omelets were said to be "juicy, golden, succulent and, above all, hot." Most visitors to Mont Saint-Michel considered a visit to her bistro a highlight of the trip. "To this day the hotel guest book testifies to the great number of national and international celebrities who stopped at Mère Poulard's."

A soufflé omelet sounds all fancy and complicated, and it does indeed require a little more work, but it is a sound investment. For almost every soufflé omelet, as for soufflés themselves, the essential first step is to separate the egg whites from the yolks, to whip the whites to soft peaks, and then gently fold the whites into the beaten yolks. There are many varieties of soufflé omelets, some savory and some sweet; the latter are often prepared with or served with liqueurs or jams and jellies. The master recipe in this chapter is for a savory soufflé. Chapter 5 includes several recipes for sweet and desert soufflé omelets.

Even among omelets, the soufflé omelet is a matter of intense disagreement, not only about what, if anything, the differences are between soufflé omelets, puffy omelets, and mousselines, but also about how best to prepare one. In many treatments, soufflé omelets, sometimes called puffed or puffy omelets, are styled mousseline omelets. (Prepared properly, a soufflé omelet is more like a cloud than is a cloud—hence, "puffy" or "puffed.") Narcissa Chamberlain distinguishes the mousseline omelet from both puffy omelets ("a dry and tasteless concoction") and the "omelette soufflé." The latter contains extra egg whites and cooks in a shallow baking dish in the oven. We might also note that soufflé omelets, at least in the view of Chamberlain and other omelet traditionalists, are always dessert omelets. I understand but do not observe the distinction.

After the whites and yolks renew their acquaintance, they are transferred to the pan and finished on the stove, or alternatively in the oven or under the broiler; I describe the three basic methods here—none is better, truer, more authentic, or even easier than any other. (Well, one is easier, I think, so I have saved it for last.)

One additional word of counsel: You must eat a soufflé omelet as soon as it leaves the oven because, like a soufflé itself, it begins to deflate as it cools.

2 eggs
1 tablespoon water
1 ½ teaspoons finely chopped fresh flat-leaf parsley, plus more for garnish
1 ½ teaspoons finely chopped fresh tarragon, plus more for garnish
½ teaspoon finely chopped fresh chives, plus more for garnish
½ teaspoon finely chopped fresh chervil, plus more for garnish
Salt and freshly ground black pepper
1 tablespoon unsalted butter
Fresh herbs for garnish
Orange slice or fresh berries for garnish

Separate the eggs. Mix the yolks with the water, parsley, tarragon, chives, chervil, salt, and pepper, until the yolks are light and pale.

Whip the egg whites in a separate bowl with a pinch of salt until soft peaks form. Do not overmix the egg whites. (Overmixing parches the whites and makes the finished omelet dry.) Gently fold the whites into the yolks, taking care not to deflate the egg whites; their volume helps keep the omelet fluffy.

Preheat a nonstick, 8- or 9-inch skillet over medium to medium-high heat.

Melt the butter in the skillet, swirl to coat the pan, and when the butter bubbles and sizzles but is not smoking or brown, pour the eggs into the pan.

Let the eggs sit quietly for about 10 seconds. Then, grabbing the handle of the pan and using a spatula, stir the eggs in the pan. At the same time, using crisp, short motions, keep the skillet moving back and forth.

When the bottom of the eggs begin to set, lower the heat to medium-low and let the omelet cook until the eggs cook through and the bottom of the omelet turns a light or golden brown, 4 to 5 minutes. If the top of the eggs seem not to finish, you can speed things along by covering the pan with a lid for about 1 minute.

If you like, you can fold the omelet in half, as if an American omelet, or you can serve it open-faced.

Slide the omelet onto a warm plate. If your omelet resists, give it a slight shove with your spatula.

Garnish with fresh herbs and a slice of orange or fresh berries.

Variation: This mousseline omelet (it uses an equal number of yolks and whites and cooks on the stove) is a good start for any savory omelet. Soufflé omelets make a great "base" for savory sauces and toppings. A little sautéed spinach, enhanced with freshly grated nutmeg and herbs, makes a great lunch or dinner for company.

Soufflé Omelette aux fines herbes under the Broiler

To make a soufflé omelet under the broiler, use the same ingredients as you would on the stove. This is my preferred method for making soufflé omelets with grated cheese. Add the cheese just before the omelet goes under the broiler. This recipe doubles nicely in a larger skillet.

Preheat the broiler.

Separate the eggs. Mix the yolks with the water, parsley, tarragon, chives, chervil, salt, and pepper, until the yolks are light and pale.

Whip the egg whites in a separate bowl with a pinch of salt until soft peaks form. Do not overmix the egg whites. (Overmixing parches the whites and makes the finished omelet dry.) Gently fold the whites into the yolks, taking care not to deflate the egg whites; their volume helps keep the omelet fluffy.

Preheat a nonstick, ovenproof 8- or 9-inch skillet over medium heat.

Melt the butter in the skillet, swirl to coat the pan, and when the butter bubbles and sizzles but is not smoking or brown, pour the eggs into the pan.

Let the eggs sit quietly for about 2 to 3 minutes, until the bottom of the omelet just begins to turn light brown.

Gently run a spatula around the edges of the omelet to make sure it is not sticking, and then place it under the broiler. The omelet is ready when it is puffy and starts to turn brown on top. Keep a close eye; this should take no more than a couple of minutes.

recipe continues . . .

Turn out the omelet onto a warm plate and garnish with fresh herbs. I like to serve this version of a soufflé omelet open-faced, like a frittata.

Soufflé Omelette aux fines herbes in the Oven

Using nearly the same method, you can make a soufflé omelet in the oven. This recipe also doubles nicely in a larger skillet.

Preheat the oven to 375°F.

Separate the eggs. Mix the yolks with the water, parsley, tarragon, chives, chervil, salt and pepper, until the yolks are light and pale.

Whip the egg whites in a separate bowl with a pinch of salt until soft peaks form. Do not overmix the egg whites. (Overmixing parches the whites and makes the finished omelet dry.) Gently fold the whites into the yolks, taking care not to deflate the egg whites; their volume helps keep the omelet fluffy.

Preheat a nonstick, ovenproof 8- or 9-inch skillet over medium heat.

Melt the butter in the skillet, swirl to coat the pan, and when the butter bubbles and sizzles but is not smoking or brown, pour the eggs into the pan.

Let the eggs sit quietly for about a minute. Gently run a spatula around the edges of the omelet to make sure it is not sticking, and then place the skillet in the oven.

Bake the omelet for about 4 to 5 minutes. The omelet is finished when the top of the eggs have set and are spongy.

Invert the omelet onto a warm plate so the browned side is visible and garnish with parsley and finely chopped chives.

A TIP FROM MY MOTHER: Sweet soufflé omelets require only a few small changes: Add a tablespoon of sugar, or a teaspoon of almond extract, to the egg whites, and a teaspoon of fresh lemon juice instead of water to the yolks. Chapter 5 includes several recipes for sweet soufflé omelets, which are often made with jams or flambéed with a sweet liqueur.

Chapter Two: Breakfast Omelets

———◦❙◉❙◦———

What nicer thing can you do for somebody than make them breakfast?

—ANTHONY BOURDAIN

If philosophy is a way of life, then the morning meal is a philosophy. Perhaps, like Jean-Paul Sartre, your waking philosophy is that "Hell is other people at breakfast." Maybe, as is the case for some of my colleagues in academia, your philosophy of breakfast is that what you eat is so important you simply must share it on social media: Hence, the website Academic Breakfast, which invites professors to post a photograph of their breakfast, to answer questions about it, and to summarize their philosophy of food in ten words or less.

Other than professors, who has the time to eat breakfast, much less take a picture of it? An omelet might seem too much bother on a workday, when there is hardly enough clock to grab a coffee and a donut at the drive-through. An omelet takes no longer, you are sure to get what you ordered, and it is better for body and spirit. Moreover, if you must tell others about your breakfast, an omelet makes a much more impressive picture than a muffin on Twittergram or Instatweet.

An omelet is also the perfect dish for a stylish weekend brunch for company, if, unlike Sartre, you enjoy guests. Most omelets are inexpensive, making it a small matter to offer guests a great variety of choices. But it is also true that some omelets, such as an Omelette Monselet (page 000), are spectacularly indulgent. Preparing an omelet for a guest, instead of just eggs, as Alice B. Toklas observed, is a mark of affection and respect.

In this chapter, I present a wide variety of recipes for breakfast omelets, from classics, such as an Omelette aux fines herbes and an Omelette Parmentier (with fresh parsley and diced potato sautéed in butter), to a spicy omelet with jalapeño bacon, plum tomatoes, and sour cream. Although I have organized the recipes in this chapter and the next into breakfast and luncheon/dinner omelets, the distinction, like so many omelet rules, is mostly an academic exercise. Indeed, in France, omelets are more common at midday or in the evening than they are at breakfast.

Omelet with Artichoke Hearts and Tomatoes

Omelette Monselet

Named in honor of Charles Monselet, a French novelist known to his contemporaries as "the king of the gastronomes," this is an elegant, indulgent omelet, perfect for visiting royalty or a holiday. Many recipes call for artichoke hearts, sometimes marinated in cream, sliced truffles, and to be served with a beef-infused tomato sauce or a demi-glace. This recipe uses a simple tomato concassée to offset the richness of the artichokes, but I might go with a more elaborate sauce for lunch or dinner. Many of the older recipes call for a flat omelet, but my version uses a classic rolled omelet as its foundation.

....

SERVES 1

Master Technique: French/Rolled

4 ounces (about half of an 8-ounce jar) artichoke hearts, drained and diced
1 teaspoon olive oil
2 eggs, mixed
1 ½ teaspoons finely chopped fresh flat-leaf parsley
1 tablespoon water
2 or 3 drops Tabasco
Salt and freshly ground black pepper
1 tablespoon unsalted butter, plus a pat for garnish
1 recipe Tomato Concassée (recipe follows)

Preheat a nonstick, 8- or 9-inch skillet over medium to medium-high heat. Sauté the diced artichoke hearts in 1 teaspoon of olive oil until they are tender and pungent. Remove and keep warm.

recipe continues . . .

Whisk the eggs, parsley, water, Tabasco, salt, and pepper with a fork until just combined. Stop when the eggs just begin to foam, 15 to 20 seconds.

Melt the butter in the skillet, swirl to coat the pan, and when the butter bubbles and sizzles, pour the eggs into the pan.

Let the eggs sit undisturbed for about 5 seconds. With a fork or a spatula, move the eggs in a circular pattern, moving the eggs from the outside of the pan to the inside. At the same time, using sharp, short, and controlled motions, keep the skillet moving back and forth.

After the eggs have begun to form curds, but before they stiffen completely, perhaps 10 seconds, remove the pan from the heat.

Add the artichoke hearts to the center of the eggs.

Use the fork to "roll" the eggs from the far side of the pan to the side closest to you. Do not let the eggs brown or stiffen.

Grab underneath the handle of the pan with the palm of your hand, thumb on top of the handle, and tilt the pan toward the plate. Invert the omelet, seam side down, onto the plate.

Dress the omelet with a thin pat of butter and sauce it with the tomato concassée.

. . . .

Variations: Recipes for Omelette Monselet often include truffles, or even goose liver. Many substitute asparagus tips for the artichoke. The sauce varies quite a bit as well. Some recipes advise a reduction of truffles; others favor a tomato and cream sauce; and still others, a béchamel.

. . . .

Tomato Concassée

A concassée is a simple sauce of peeled, seeded, and chopped fresh tomatoes. Serve it raw, with perhaps a little olive oil and salt, or balsamic vinegar. Or you can reduce the sauce on the stove, which intensifies the flavor. What sorts of seasonings, and how much, should be added depends on the quality of the tomatoes. This recipe is for a very simple, honest concassée. It goes wonderfully with a great variety of other dishes, including, of course, pasta, as well as chicken, pork, and fish.

....

2 medium plum tomatoes
Salt and freshly ground black pepper
Olive oil (optional)
1 tablespoon chopped fresh basil (optional)

With a sharp knife, score a shallow X-shaped mark on the nonstem side of the tomatoes.

Prepare an ice water bath. Place one tomato at a time into a pot of gently boiling water. (This is "blanching," or "shocking," the tomato.) When the cut sides of the X begin just to curl (this takes about 20 seconds, but it will depend on how ripe the tomato is), remove the tomato and place it immediately in the ice water bath.

When the tomatoes are no longer hot to the touch, remove them from the ice water bath and set them on a cutting board. The skin should peel off easily.

Cut the peeled tomatoes in half and remove the seeds. Cut the tomatoes into small dice. Place them in a bowl and season with salt and pepper.

Concassée makes a wonderful sauce for an omelet just as it is, but you can gussy it up by cooking the concassée in a little olive oil and by adding a few other ingredients of your choice, such as fresh herbs, a fine balsamic vinegar, or minced garlic.

Chipped Beef Omelet

I think of chipped beef on toast as a fairly old-fashioned dish, perhaps because I haven't seen it on a menu in many years. This was my father's favorite omelet. I had completely forgotten about how much my father loved chipped beef until I ran across the recipe in Marjorie Mosser's classic cookbook *Good Maine Food*. I've changed Mosser's recipe just a little, to make it suitable for one person. My father did not have much to say about omelets, but he insisted that chipped beef, whether in an omelet or not, must always be served with white toast.

....

SERVES 1
Master Technique: American/Folded

1 cup chipped beef
1 cup White Sauce (page 000)
Salt and freshly ground black pepper
2 eggs, mixed
1 tablespoon heavy cream
1 tablespoon unsalted butter

Combine the chipped beef and the white sauce. Season with salt and pepper.

Preheat a nonstick, 8- or 9-inch skillet over medium to medium-high heat.

Whisk the eggs, cream, salt, and pepper with a fork until just combined.

Melt the butter in the skillet, swirl to coat the pan, and when the butter sizzles, add the eggs. Swirl the eggs so they cover the entire bottom of the pan. Let the eggs sit quietly for about 10 seconds.

Holding the handle of the pan and using a spatula, pull the uncooked egg toward the center of the pan, proceeding calmly and deliberately around the compass, north to south to east to west. Use a spatula to lift the eggs from the rim of the pan, and move the remaining uncooked egg under the cooked portion.

Let the omelet cook for a minute or two, occasionally moving the uncooked egg under the cooked portion as necessary.

Cover the eggs with half of the chipped beef mixture.

Fold the omelet in half, moving from the outside of the pan to the inside.

Turn out the omelet onto a warm plate. Spoon the remaining chipped beef mixture over the omelet and serve immediately.

. . . .

Variation: Although it was once very popular (and a staple in school cafeterias, particularly in the Northeast and mid-Atlantic United States), chipped beef can be difficult to find; it usually comes in small glass jars. A good alternative is crumbled pork sausage in a white sauce, what many folks would call sausage gravy.

. . . .

Denver Omelet

One wonderful summer, while in college, I worked as a short-order cook on the coast of Maine. I must have made a hundred "Denvers," as we called them, although sometimes someone would ask for a western or a southwestern or a Spanish omelet and momentarily confuse both the waitstaff and the kitchen. I concluded my time there convinced, and I still am, that a Denver/western/southwestern/Spanish is the most popular omelet in the United States. Its provenance, though, is a matter of some uncertainty. Some folks, including James Beard, think it was originally a sort of scrambled egg sandwich invented by Chinese cooks working in logging camps and on the transcontinental railway, who adapted the traditional Chinese dish of egg foo yong to bread. This might also explain why it was called a "western" and why it later became a "Denver."

When I was a young boy, my grandfather would take me early in the morning to the local diner (Jimmy's) in Auburn, Maine. Without exception, Gramps would order a Denver sandwich, a Denver omelet on white toast. Always, without exception, the waitress would sing out: "One western on white." I can't imagine eating a Denver without cradling it between two pieces of perfectly toasted white bread.

....

SERVES 1
Master Technique: American/Folded

2 tablespoons diced yellow onion
2 tablespoons diced red bell pepper
2 tablespoons diced green bell pepper
Unsalted butter
2 tablespoons (about 1½ ounces) julienned ham
Salt and freshly ground black pepper
2 eggs, mixed
1 tablespoon water
2 or 3 drops Tabasco
Melon slice or fanned strawberry for garnish

Sauté the onion and bell pepper in butter until the vegetables are soft, but do not brown them. Add the ham to the onion and peppers and cook until warm. Season with salt and pepper.

Preheat a nonstick, 8- or 9-inch skillet over medium to medium-high heat.

Whisk the eggs, onion, bell pepper, ham, water, Tabasco, salt, and black pepper with a fork until just combined.

Melt 1 tablespoon of butter in the skillet, swirl to coat the pan, and when the butter sizzles, add the eggs. Swirl the eggs so they cover the entire bottom of the pan. Let the eggs sit quietly for about 10 seconds.

Holding the handle of the pan and using a spatula, pull the uncooked egg toward the center of the pan, proceeding calmly and deliberately around the compass, north to south to east to west. Use a spatula to lift the eggs from the rim of the pan, and move the remaining uncooked egg under the cooked portion.

Let the omelet cook for a minute or two, occasionally moving the uncooked egg under the cooked portion as necessary.

Fold the omelet in half, moving from the outside of the pan to the inside.

Turn out the omelet onto a warm plate. Garnish with a slice of melon or a fanned strawberry, and serve immediately.

Variations: A Denver is not really a Denver if it doesn't include onions, bell peppers, and ham, but that doesn't mean it is not a Denver if you add something else to the mix. Common additions include cheese, mushrooms, spicy peppers, such as jalapeño, and even pico de gallo.

Egg White, Baby Spinach, Plum Tomato, and Garlic Omelet

Sadly, egg white omelets have a lot to apologize for. Often they are insipid, pale and colorless, and almost as often, they are dry and tasteless. If one takes a little care, however, egg whites make an admirable and versatile palate for the creative cook. The secret to a delicious egg white omelet is to take the egg whites as they are, not to pretend that they are no different from whole eggs. This version of an egg white omelet thus bends some of the ordinary rules for omelets—we whip the whites longer than we would otherwise, to get more air and volume into them (as we might for a puffy or a mousseline omelet) and cook them over a lower flame. We overcome their pallor with brightly colored vegetables. An egg white omelet also needs a little help to make it look appealing on the plate. I usually reserve a bit of the vegetables to spoon over the top of the omelet. You can maintain much of the healthy benefit of this egg white omelet if you use three whites and a single yolk. You might also try replacing the tablespoon of water with a teaspoon of a flavored vinegar.

SERVES 1

Master Technique: Soufflé

½ cup baby spinach leaves
1 tablespoon plus 1 teaspoon olive oil
2 tablespoons seeded and diced plum tomato
1 teaspoon minced garlic
4 egg whites
1 tablespoon water
2 or 3 drops Tabasco
Salt and freshly ground black pepper
1 tablespoon grated Ricotta Salata or Pecorino Romano for garnish

Sauté the baby spinach in 1 teaspoon of the olive oil until gently wilted. Add the plum tomato and garlic and when warm, remove from the heat. Season to taste.

Preheat a nonstick, 8- to 9-inch skillet over medium-low heat.

Whisk the egg whites with the water, Tabasco, salt, and pepper with a fork until they are very frothy and almost form soft peaks. We want the whites to increase in volume by incorporating air, which helps keep the omelet fluffy.

Heat the remaining tablespoon of oil over medium to medium-low heat. Swirl to coat the pan, and when it shimmers, add the eggs. Let the eggs sit still for about 10 seconds. Holding the handle of the pan and using a spatula, and moving north to south, east to west, pull the uncooked egg toward the center of the pan. Use a spatula to lift eggs from the rim of the pan and to move any uncooked egg under cooked portion.

Add the spinach mixture to the center of the eggs. Fold the omelet in half, moving from the outside of the pan to the inside.

Invert the omelet, seam side down, onto the plate. Garnish with the grated Ricotta Salata.

Variation: Egg whites take well to bold flavors. One of my favorite egg white omelets incorporates wild mushrooms, lightly sautéed in olive oil, and a variety of hot peppers, such as red and green jalapeños, or brightly colored bell peppers. Garnish with pico de gallo and a sprig of cilantro.

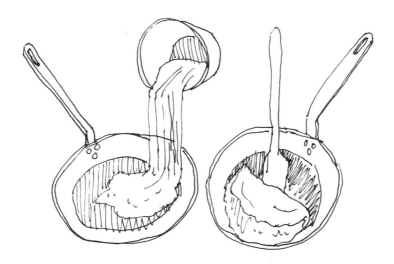

Ellery's Cheese Omelet

I almost did not include a recipe for a cheese omelet in this book because after all, who really needs a recipe for a cheese omelet? Make an omelet. Add cheese. Done. But I like cheese. Who *doesn't* like cheese? Processed faux cheese wrapped in plastic, cheese in a spray can, cheese cubes on a stick, cow's milk, sheep's milk, goat cheeses, yak cheeses, artisanal cheeses, PDO, PGI, and TSG cheeses. I love them all and they all make for great omelets. The thorniest thing about a cheese omelet is when to add the cheese. How much cheese you should use partly depends on the cheese itself, but assuming you are using a high-quality hard cheese, 2 tablespoons for 2 eggs is a good rule of thumb. By the way, I named this recipe for my daughter, Ellery. If you read closely, you will see that it does not have to include any cheese. Ellery *hates* cheese. Which is why I named this cheese omelet after her.

SERVES 1
Master Technique: American/Folded

2 eggs, mixed
1 tablespoon water
2 or 3 drops Tabasco
Salt and freshly ground black pepper
1 tablespoon unsalted butter
1 tablespoon grated Parmigiano-Reggiano (optional)
1 tablespoon grated Gruyère (optional)
2 tablespoons (about 25 grams) very finely diced croutons
Cheese triangle for garnish
Melon slice or fanned strawberry for garnish

Preheat a nonstick, 8- or 9-inch skillet over medium to medium-high heat.

Whisk the eggs, water, Tabasco, salt, and pepper with a fork until just combined.

Melt the butter in the skillet, swirl to coat the pan, and when the butter sizzles, add the eggs. Swirl the eggs so they cover the entire bottom of the pan. Let the eggs sit quietly for about 10 seconds.

Holding the handle of the pan and using a spatula, pull the uncooked egg toward the center of the pan, proceeding calmly and deliberately around the compass, north to south to east to west. Use a spatula to lift the eggs from the rim of the pan, and move the remaining uncooked egg under the cooked portion.

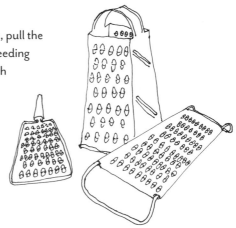

Add the Parmigiano-Reggiano and Gruyère (if using) and the croutons to the center of the eggs. If you do not like cheese, this is the place where you should omit it.

Fold the omelet in half, moving from the outside of the pan to the inside. Turn out the omelet onto a warm plate. Garnish with a triangle of cheese on the top of the omelet (or don't) and a slice of melon or a fanned strawberry.

Variations: How many kinds of cheese are there? Cheeses that melt smoothly and do not overwhelm the palate, such as Gruyère, are a good choice for omelets, as are fine Cheddars. Goat cheeses take especially well to omelets, too. You may be surprised to find how easy it is to find local producers of high-quality, artisanal cheeses near you. A farmers' market is a good place to begin.

One of the most unusual recipes I have ever seen for a cheese omelet appears in Marjorie Mosser's *Good Maine Food*. It calls for a teaspoon of gin to help make the omelet fluffy. I do not know whether vodka or tequila would work as well, but I take seriously the practice of the noted philosopher W. C. Fields never to drink "anything stronger than gin before breakfast."

Many Mushrooms Omelet

Please take advantage of the wonderful variety of mushrooms you are likely to find at even the least adventuresome of supermarkets. Each variety has a unique texture and taste. Some are brash and musky; others are subtle and sweet. Some mushrooms are earthy; others are delicate. This recipe calls for cremini, shiitake, and morels, all of which are now easy to find. They are only suggestions. If you see baby portobellos, oyster mushrooms, or chanterelles, please try them.

Mushrooms do need a cleaning before you cook them, but they certainly do not need a full bath. Brush them gently with a clean towel, slice or chop them, and then into a hot pan with butter or oil they should go. Make sure the pan is hot. We want the mushrooms to cook quickly and to turn brown. Most mushrooms are naturally watery. If cooked too slowly, they release their moisture and steam in the pan instead of frying. (Steamed mushrooms are steel gray and rubbery. You don't want them in your omelet or in anything else.) After the mushrooms take on a nice brown color, you can add a scant tablespoon of a good, flavored vinegar, if desired, and season with salt and pepper.

....

SERVES 1
Master Technique: American/Folded

¼ pound mushrooms, sliced (about 1 cup, depending on the variety of mushroom),
    2 tablespoons reserved for garnish
1 teaspoon olive oil
1 tablespoon minced garlic
Salt and freshly ground black pepper
2 eggs, mixed
1 tablespoon water
2 or 3 drops Tabasco
1 tablespoon unsalted butter
Sprig of something green for garnish

Preheat a nonstick, 8- or 9-inch skillet over medium to medium-high heat.

Sauté the mushrooms in the olive oil over medium-high heat until they are deep brown. Add the garlic, salt, and pepper, and set aside. A cup of mushrooms might seem like a lot, but when cooked the yield will be about ⅓ cup, and you will want to save some of the cooked mushrooms for a garnish.

Whisk the eggs, water, Tabasco, salt, and pepper with a fork until just combined.

Melt the butter in the skillet, swirl to coat the pan, and when the butter sizzles, add the eggs. Swirl the eggs so they cover the entire bottom of the pan. Let the eggs sit quietly for about 10 seconds.

Holding the handle of the pan and using a spatula, pull the uncooked egg toward the center of the pan, proceeding calmly and deliberately around the compass, north to south to east to west. Use a spatula to lift the eggs from the rim of the pan, and move the remaining uncooked egg under the cooked portion.

Add the mushrooms to the center of the eggs, reserving a tablespoon or two for the garnish.

Fold the omelet in half, moving from the outside of the pan to the inside.

Turn out the omelet onto a warm plate. Garnish with the remaining mushrooms and a sprig of something green.

Variations: Mushrooms pair exceptionally well with broiled or slow-roasted tomatoes, green leafy vegetables, such as kale and collards, and with cheeses.

Omelet with Fines Herbes

Omelette aux fines herbes

This omelet was Narcissa Chamberlain's idea of the perfect omelet, and she may well have been right. No collection of omelet recipes could be complete or even respectable without a recipe for an Omelette aux fines herbes. In the canonical version, which I follow here, the recipe calls for finely chopped fresh herbs (dried simply will not do). If there is any argument about its preparation, it consists in the tantalizing question of how much of each herb one should include. There is no question at all, however, that the classical recipe must use parsley, tarragon, chives, and chervil. Anything else is . . . probably something quite wonderful, but not an Omelette aux fines herbes.

....

SERVES 1
Master Technique: French/Rolled

2 eggs, mixed
1 tablespoon water
1 ½ teaspoons finely chopped fresh flat-leaf parsley, plus more for garnish
1 ½ teaspoons finely chopped fresh tarragon, plus more for garnish
½ teaspoon finely chopped fresh chives, plus more for garnish
½ teaspoon finely chopped fresh chervil, plus more for garnish
Salt and freshly ground black pepper
1 tablespoon unsalted butter, plus a pat for garnish

Preheat a nonstick, 8- or 9-inch skillet over medium to medium-high heat.

Whisk the eggs, water, parsley, tarragon, chives, chervil, salt, and pepper with a fork until just combined. Stop when the eggs just begin to foam, 15 to 20 seconds.

Melt the butter in the skillet, swirl to coat the pan, and when the butter bubbles and sizzles, pour the eggs into the pan.

Let the eggs sit undisturbed for about 5 seconds. With a fork or a spatula, move the eggs in a circular pattern, moving the eggs from the outside of the pan to the inside. At the same time, using sharp, short, and controlled motions, keep the skillet moving back and forth.

After the eggs have begun to form curds, but before they stiffen completely, perhaps 10 seconds, remove the pan from the heat and use the fork to "roll" the eggs from the far side of the pan to the side closest to you. Do not let the eggs brown or stiffen.

Grab underneath the handle of the pan with the palm of your hand, thumb on top of the handle, and tilt the pan to the plate. Invert the omelet, seam side down, onto the plate.

Dress the omelet with a thin pat of butter and garnish with some of the reserved fines herbes.

Variations: The simplest and most common variation on this omelet is to add different herbs to the mix. You will be surprised at how this single change can dramatically alter the taste. I am especially fond of marjoram, sage, basil, and savory. Some other herbs, such as rosemary, dill, and cilantro, seem to me to overwhelm the eggs, but your taste will be unique.

Simple Omelet with Potatoes, Onion, and Bacon

Omelette bonne femme

Anything styled *bonne femme* in French cooking signifies a dish prepared casually, or in the manner of a "good wife." *Cuisine de bonne femme* is thus a style of cooking that stresses integrity, economy, and the honesty of fresh, local ingredients. By custom, an Omelette à la bonne femme is prepared with potatoes, onion, and bacon (or, very traditionally, salt pork). Many a bonne femme would add parsley or cheese. Some recipes dress the omelet with a light cream sauce—perhaps better for a brunch or luncheon than for a light breakfast.

....

SERVES 1
Master Recipe: French/Rolled

2 eggs, mixed
1 tablespoon water
2 or 3 drops Tabasco
1 tablespoon finely chopped fresh flat-leaf parsley, plus more for garnish
Salt and freshly ground black pepper
1 tablespoon unsalted butter, plus a pat for garnish
¼ cup boiled, cooled, and finely diced white or red potato
4 to 6 slices bacon, cooked and chopped (about ⅓ cup)

Preheat a nonstick, 8- or 9-inch skillet over medium to medium-high heat.

Whisk the eggs, water, Tabasco, parsley, salt, and pepper with a fork until just combined. Stop when the eggs just begin to foam, 15 to 20 seconds.

Melt the butter in the skillet, swirl to coat the pan, and when the butter bubbles and sizzles, pour the eggs into the pan.

Let the eggs sit undisturbed for about 5 seconds. With a fork or a spatula, move the eggs in a circular pattern, moving the eggs from the outside of the pan to the inside.

At the same time, using sharp, short, and controlled motions, keep the skillet moving back and forth.

After the eggs have begun to form curds, but before they stiffen completely, perhaps 10 seconds, add the potato and all but 1 teaspoon of the bacon to the center of the pan.

Remove the pan from the heat and use the fork to "roll" the eggs from the far side of the pan to the side closest to you. Do not let the eggs brown or stiffen.

Grab underneath the handle of the pan with the palm of your hand, thumb on top of the handle, and tilt the pan toward the plate. Invert the omelet, seam side down, onto the plate.

Dress the omelet with a thin pat of butter and garnish with some of the parsley and the remaining bacon.

Variations: One of the wonderful things about bonne femme as a style of cooking is that it is very casual. This omelet, for example, takes beautifully to the addition of a small bit of grated cheese or to various greens, such as baby spinach or arugula.

A TIP FROM MY MOTHER: Cook the bacon first, and reserve the bacon fat. Instead of boiling the potatoes, dice them finely and sauté them in the bacon fat. When the potatoes are nearly finished, add a chopped garlic clove and remove the pan from the heat. Drain the potatoes in a colander.

Simple Omelet
with Croutons and Chives
Omelette grand-mère

Any dish prepared *à la grand-mère* means, of course, that is prepared just like someone (else's) grandmother used to make it. On some occasions, though, it can be a mark of derision. Do you remember the story of Pierre Franey's ill-fated omelet? The chef who had asked Franey to prepare the omelet, a sous chef named Domas, threw the specimen at Franey, exclaiming, "That's no omelette aux fines herbes, that's an omelette grand-mère," a disparaging reference to the wrinkles in the omelet.

Just about every recipe for an Omelette grand-mère includes croutons or bits of bread, often left over from last night's supper, sautéed in butter. Dishes cooked *à la grand-mère* are not pretentious or fancy, so there is no need to buy fresh bread or a *pain festive* for croutons. But slices from a nice baguette do make very nice croutons.

....

SERVES 1
Master Technique: French/Rolled

2 eggs, mixed
1 ½ teaspoons finely chopped fresh flat-leaf parsley
1 ½ teaspoons finely chopped fresh chives, plus more stalks for garnish
1 tablespoon water
2 or 3 drops Tabasco
Salt and freshly ground black pepper
1 tablespoon unsalted butter, plus a pat for garnish
2 tablespoons toasted, very finely diced croutons

Preheat a nonstick, 8- or 9-inch skillet over medium to medium-high heat.

Whisk the eggs, parsley, chives, water, Tabasco, salt, and pepper with a fork until just combined. Stop when the eggs just begin to foam, about 15 to 20 seconds.

Melt the butter in the skillet, swirl to coat the pan, and when the butter bubbles and sizzles, pour the eggs into the pan.

Let the eggs sit undisturbed for about 5 seconds. With a fork or a spatula, move the eggs in a circular pattern, moving the eggs from the outside of the pan to the inside. At the same time, using sharp, short, and controlled motions, keep the skillet moving back and forth.

After the eggs have begun to form curds, but before they stiffen completely, perhaps 10 seconds, remove the pan from the heat.

Add the croutons to the eggs, reserving a few for garnish.

Use the fork to "roll" the eggs from the far side of the pan to the side closest to you. Do not let the eggs brown or stiffen.

Grab underneath the handle of the pan with the palm of your hand, thumb on top of the handle, and tilt the pan toward the plate. Invert the omelet, seam side down, onto the plate.

Dress the omelet with a thin pat of butter and garnish with the reserved croutons and a few stalks of chives.

> **A TIP FROM MY MOTHER:** If you are making many croutons, it is easier to toast them in the oven than to sauté them on the stove; simply drizzle the bread crumbs with butter to achieve a similar taste. Consider seasoning your croutons with various spices, such as sage, rosemary, thyme, paprika, or garlic powder.

Omelet with Diced Potatoes

Omelette Parmentier

In French cuisine, *parmentier* means with potatoes, although this term is not the French word for potato (which is *pomme de terre*). This is instead yet another example of an honorific omelet, named, aptly, for Antoine-Augustin Parmentier, a celebrated botanist and vocal advocate of the potato. Prior to Parmentier's saintly work on its behalf, the potato was deeply distrusted in France, and indeed, thought by some to cause leprosy. (It doesn't.) Escoffier's version of an Omelette Parmentier is still the classic, and I vary from it below only in one or two inconsequential respects.

....

Serves 1
Master Technique: French/Rolled

2 eggs, mixed
1 ½ teaspoons finely chopped fresh flat-leaf parsley, plus more for garnish
1 tablespoon water
2 or 3 drops Tabasco
Salt and freshly ground black pepper
1 tablespoon unsalted butter, plus a pat for garnish
¼ cup boiled, cooled, and finely diced white or red potato

Preheat a nonstick, 8- or 9-inch skillet over medium to medium-high heat.

Whisk the eggs, parsley, water, Tabasco, salt, and pepper with a fork until just combined. Stop when the eggs just begin to foam, 15 to 20 seconds.

Melt the butter in the skillet, swirl to coat the pan, and when the butter bubbles and sizzles, pour the eggs into the pan.

Let the eggs sit undisturbed for about 5 seconds. With a fork or a spatula, move the eggs in a circular pattern, moving the eggs from the outside of the pan to the inside. At the same time, using sharp, short, and controlled motions, keep the skillet moving back and forth.

After the eggs have begun to form curds, but before they stiffen completely, perhaps 10 seconds, remove the pan from the heat. Add the potatoes to the center of the eggs.

Use the fork to "roll" the eggs from the far side of the pan to the side closest to you. Do not let the eggs brown or stiffen.

Grab underneath the handle of the pan with the palm of your hand, thumb on top of the handle, and tilt the pan toward the plate. Invert the omelet, seam side down, onto the plate.

Dress the omelet with a thin pat of butter and garnish with chopped parsley.

Variation: Many of the older recipes for this omelet call for a flat omelet, but this recipe has a classic rolled omelet as its foundation. Small red potatoes, with their skin on, add color to the dish.

A TIP FROM MY MOTHER: Instead of boiling the potatoes, sauté them in bacon fat; it is not traditional, but it adds flavor.

Bacon, Cheese, and Mustard Omelet

Omelette Piora

This very unusual but delicious omelet combines diced bacon, Swiss, and, crucially, a good French mustard. *Piora* means to "blossom" in Korean, but nothing about this omelet, which I first encountered in Narcissa Chamberlain's *The Omelette Book*, even remotely suggests anything Korean. A more likely source for the name is the cheese, perhaps a nod to the Val Piora in the Ticino region of southern Switzerland. Mustard makes this omelet. Use a good mustard, and do not be afraid to try one of the many specialty mustards on the market. My favorite is a very coarsely ground wasabi mustard available from Stonewall Kitchens, in York, Maine. You might also consider substituting fresh horseradish for the mustard.

....

SERVES 1
Master Technique: American/Folded

2 eggs, mixed
1 tablespoon Dijon mustard
Salt and freshly ground black pepper
1 tablespoon unsalted butter
3 to 4 slices bacon, cooked and chopped (about ⅓ cup)
2 tablespoons shredded Swiss, plus a triangle of cheese for garnish

---

Preheat a nonstick, 8- or 9-inch skillet over medium to medium-high heat.

Whisk the eggs, mustard, salt, and pepper with a fork until just combined.

Melt the butter in the skillet, swirl to coat the pan, and when the butter sizzles, add the eggs. Swirl the eggs so they cover the entire bottom of the pan. Let the eggs sit quietly for about 10 seconds.

Holding the handle of the pan and using a spatula, pull the uncooked egg toward the center of the pan, proceeding calmly and deliberately around the compass, north to south to east to west. Use a spatula to lift the eggs from the rim of the pan, and move the remaining uncooked egg under the cooked portion.

Let the omelet cook for a minute or two, occasionally moving the uncooked egg under the cooked portion as necessary.

Add the bacon and cheese to the center of the eggs.

Using a spatula, fold the omelet in half, moving from the outside of the pan to the inside. Turn out the omelet onto a warm plate. Garnish with a triangle of cheese on the top of the omelet.

Omelet with Jalapeño Bacon, Plum Tomatoes, and Sour Cream

Count me a devoted congregant in the Church of Bacon. We are fortunate indeed to be living in a bacon renaissance, when it is easy to find high quality and specialty bacons at many stores. This recipe uses one of my favorites—a smoked bacon cured with jalapeño peppers. It is also surprisingly easy to make your own flavored bacon, either from scratch or by taking a high-quality store-bought bacon and marinating it or adding other ingredients (coarsely ground black pepper!) to it and slow cooking it in the oven.

....

SERVES 1
Master Technique: American/Folded

2 eggs, mixed
1 tablespoon water
2 or 3 drops Tabasco
Salt and freshly ground black pepper
1 tablespoon unsalted butter
3 to 4 slices bacon, cooked and chopped (about ⅓ cup)
2 tablespoons seeded and diced plum tomato
1 generous tablespoon sour cream for garnish
Cilantro sprig for garnish

Preheat a nonstick, 8- or 9-inch skillet over medium to medium-high heat.

Whisk the eggs, water, Tabasco, salt, and pepper with a fork until just combined.

Melt the butter in the skillet, swirl to coat the pan, and when the butter sizzles, add the eggs. Swirl the eggs so they cover the entire bottom of the pan. Let the eggs sit quietly for about 10 seconds.

Holding the handle of the pan and using a spatula, pull the uncooked egg toward the center of the pan, proceeding calmly and deliberately around the compass, north to south to east to west. Use a spatula to lift the eggs from the rim of the pan, and move the remaining uncooked egg under the cooked portion.

Let the omelet cook for a minute or two, occasionally moving the uncooked egg under the cooked portion as necessary.

Add the bacon and the tomato to the center of the eggs, reserving a teaspoon of each to garnish.

Using a spatula, fold the omelet in half, moving from the outside of the pan to the inside. Turn out the omelet onto a warm plate.

Garnish with the reserved bacon and tomato, plus the sour cream and cilantro.

Variations: Good bacon now comes in a variety of tastes and flavors. I am very fond of black pepper bacon, for example, which is a superb substitute in this recipe. You might also improve the sour cream with fresh lime juice and cilantro.

Prosciutto, Parmesan, and Rosemary Omelet

A ham and cheese omelet is on every menu in every breakfast spot in the United States. It is easy to understand why: A ham and cheese omelet is comfort food, requires no fancy ingredients, and is simple to prepare. Just as important, it is predictable. One has to be in a very special mood to appreciate a surprise in the morning, but this fancy version of a familiar comfort is one of the exceptions.

Parmesan tuiles are a lovely garnish for savory omelets (recipe follows). In their place, a few curls of shaved Parmesan will work very well.

....

SERVES 1
Master Technique: American/Folded

2 eggs, mixed
1 tablespoon water
1 tablespoon chopped fresh rosemary
Salt and freshly ground black pepper
1 tablespoon unsalted butter
2 ounces prosciutto, roughly chopped
2 tablespoons shaved Parmigiano-Reggiano curls (optional)
1 recipe Parmesan Tuiles (optional; recipe follows)

Preheat a nonstick, 8- or 9-inch skillet over medium to medium-high heat.

Whisk the eggs, water, rosemary, salt, and pepper with a fork until just combined.

Melt the butter in the skillet, swirl to coat the pan, and when the butter sizzles, add the eggs. Swirl the eggs so they cover the entire bottom of the pan. Let the eggs sit quietly for about 10 seconds.

Holding the handle of the pan and using a spatula, pull the uncooked egg toward the center of the pan, proceeding calmly and deliberately around the compass, north to south to east to west. Use a spatula to lift the eggs from the rim of the pan, and move the remaining uncooked egg under the cooked portion. Add the prosciutto and cheese to the center of the eggs.

Using a spatula, fold the omelet in half, moving from the outside of the pan to the inside. Turn out the omelet onto a warm plate. Garnish with shaved Parmigiano-Reggiano curls or Parmesan tuiles and serve immediately.

Variations: I like the way rosemary pairs with prosciutto, but fresh basil and oregano would also be good choices. And any good ham (a world unto itself) will do. . . .

Parmesan Tuiles

A tuile (French for "tile") is a savory or sweet cookie baked in the oven and then cast into curved shapes that resemble the red roof tiles common in the Mediterranean. Tuiles are very simple to prepare, but they do require your attention. This recipe is for a savory cheese tuile. It is a delicious finger food (and is wonderful on salads!) and a spectacular, unusual garnish. Please do not use generic grated cheese for the tuiles or for the omelet. Nothing compares to the taste of true Parmigiano-Reggiano.

MAKES ABOUT 12 TUILES

2 cups grated Parmigiano-Reggiano cheese

Preheat the oven to 350°F. Line a cookie or baking sheet with a Silpat or parchment paper.

Spread 3 tablespoons of the cheese into a thin, circular shape and continue to create cheese disks on the pan, leaving about an inch between each tuile.

Bake until golden brown, 10 to 12 minutes. Keep a close eye—these will burn easily.

Remove the tuiles with a metal spatula. Gently bend each tuile over a rolling pin or a wine bottle. As the tuile cools, it will curve. Store in an airtight container.

Variation: Finely chopped herbs, such as rosemary or thyme, are a wonderful complement to the cheese. I sometimes add coarsely ground black pepper.

Smoked Salmon
and Goat Cheese Omelet

This is an elegant and surprisingly simple omelet, suitable for a leisurely breakfast for one person or for a romantic brunch.

....

SERVES 1
Master Technique: American/Folded

3 tablespoons sour cream or Greek yogurt
1 tablespoon coarsely ground prepared mustard
Vinegar or water, for thinning (optional)
2 eggs, mixed
1 tablespoon finely chopped chives
1½ teaspoons finely chopped fresh dill or tarragon
1 tablespoon water
Salt and freshly ground black pepper
1 tablespoon unsalted butter
¼ cup chopped smoked salmon (about 2 ounces)
2 tablespoons crumbled goat cheese
Fresh dill or chives for garnish

Combine the sour cream and mustard to make a sauce. If it is too thick, add a teaspoon of vinegar or water.

Preheat a nonstick, 8- or 9-inch skillet over medium to medium-high heat.

Whisk the eggs, chives, dill, water, salt, and pepper with a fork until just combined.

Melt the butter in the skillet, swirl to coat the pan, and when the butter sizzles, add the eggs. Swirl the eggs so they cover the entire bottom of the pan. Let the eggs sit quietly for about 10 seconds.

Holding the handle of the pan and using a spatula, pull the uncooked egg toward the center of the pan, proceeding calmly and deliberately around the compass, north to south to east to west. Use a spatula to lift the eggs from the rim of the pan, and move the remaining uncooked egg under the cooked portion.

Add the smoked salmon and 1 tablespoon of the goat cheese to the center of the eggs.

Using a spatula, fold the omelet in half, moving from the outside of the pan to the inside. Turn out the omelet onto a warm plate. Garnish with the yogurt sauce, remaining tablespoon of goat cheese, and fresh dill or chives.

Variation: This omelet pairs very nicely with a béarnaise sauce. The béarnaise is so rich, however, that I usually omit the goat cheese.

Creamed Shrimp and Crab Omelet

Seafood and omelets are an old and venerable pairing. Indeed, Narcissa's Chamberlain's definitive collection, *The Omelette Book*, includes well over 40 recipes for seafood omelets, and just about every book I have ever consulted includes some version of an omelet composed of shrimp and crab. Here is my version. You do not need to make the cream sauce that accompanies this recipe, but it makes this omelet a great choice for company or a weekend brunch.

....

SERVES 1
Master Technique: American/Folded

⅛ cup (about 1 ounce) shrimp
Salt and freshly ground black pepper
⅛ cup (about 1 ounce) crabmeat
2 eggs, mixed
1 tablespoon water
2 or 3 drops Tabasco
1 tablespoon chopped fresh flat-leaf parsley, plus more for garnish
1 tablespoon unsalted butter
2 green onions, chopped
White Sauce (recipe follows)

Sauté the shrimp, season with salt and pepper, and set aside.

Clean and shred the crabmeat, if necessary. Sauté the crabmeat until heated through, season with salt and pepper, and set aside.

Preheat a nonstick, 8- or 9-inch skillet over medium to medium-high heat.

Whisk the eggs, water, Tabasco, parsley, salt, and pepper with a fork until just combined.

Melt the butter in the skillet, swirl to coat the pan, and when the butter sizzles, add the eggs. Swirl the eggs so they cover the entire bottom of the pan. Let the eggs sit quietly for about 10 seconds.

Holding the handle of the pan and using a spatula, pull the uncooked egg toward the center of the pan, proceeding calmly and deliberately around the compass, north to south to east to west. Use a spatula to lift the eggs from the rim of the pan, and move the remaining uncooked egg under the cooked portion.

Let the omelet cook for a minute or two, occasionally moving the uncooked egg under the cooked portion as necessary.

Add half of the shrimp, all of the crabmeat, and half of the green onions to the center of the eggs.

Using a spatula, fold the omelet in half, moving from the outside of the pan to the inside.

Dress the omelet with the white sauce on a warm plate. Garnish with the remaining green onions and shrimp.

. . . .

Variations: Bay scallops (the small ones) are a nice addition to the shrimp and the crab or in place of the crab. Many folks include Gruyère or a similar cheese with seafood omelets. Broiled plum or grape tomatoes are a nice accompaniment.

This particular recipe would be quite surprising to most trained chefs and to dedicated students of the omelet. A more traditional creamed omelet requires the cook to heat the crab (any fish or shellfish will do) in a tablespoon of butter, salt, pepper, and a pinch of cayenne pepper. When the fish is hot, add about ½ teaspoon of flour, 2 tablespoons of heavy cream, and sherry to taste and stir gently. Let the fish simmer softly in the sauce for a minute. Set it aside and use it to fill the eggs after they have begun to set.

. . . .

recipe continues . . .

White Sauce

This is an uncomplicated white sauce, essential in any kitchen and remarkably versatile.

....

2 tablespoons unsalted butter
2 tablespoons all-purpose flour
1 cup whole milk or light cream
Salt and freshly ground white pepper
⅛ teaspoon cayenne pepper
⅛ teaspoon freshly grated nutmeg (optional)

Melt the butter in a small saucepot over medium-low heat.

Stir the flour into the butter with a wooden spoon, making a roux. Cook for about a minute to remove the taste of the raw flour, but do not color the roux.

Slowly pour in the milk, salt, pepper, and cayenne, and whisk vigorously until the sauce thickens. If you are using nutmeg, add it after the cream sauce has thickened. If the sauce is too thick, add a little more milk. Adjust the seasonings and keep warm.

> **A TIP FROM MY MOTHER:** I think a white sauce was the very first thing my mother taught me to cook. She was quite insistent that the sauce had "to be built slowly, from the spoon up," by which she meant that the proper way to make a white sauce was to add the milk to the flour very slowly, two tablespoons at a time, to give the sauce time to mature. My chef-instructors in culinary school were amused when I did the same, pointing out that there was no time for such nonsense in a professional kitchen. Yet Elizabeth David's recipe for Sauce Béchamel instructs one to add the milk "gradually" and to cook the sauce "very slowly, to allow the flour to cook; this precaution is frequently omitted by English cooks, hence the appalling taste of imperfectly dissolved flour." I still make a white sauce the way my mom did.

Chapter Three:
Luncheon & Dinner Omelets

---·◦─◦┤◉├◦─◦·---

Lunch kills half of Paris, supper the other half.

—ATTRIBUTED TO CHARLES DE MONTESQUIEU

Lunch is a lost art. No one has the time anymore for a leisurely lunch, and unless one thinks reheating something in a microwave is cooking, no one cooks lunch anymore. Worse, there is no one to lament the loss of lunch, whereas the passing of the family dinner appears to some folks (I am not one) to be a national crisis of monumental proportions. Cultural critics, politicians, social workers, and academic philosophers (some of whom I count as friends and whose work I respect enormously) all bemoan the passing of the family meal as a threat to the family, to our way of life, to democracy, and indeed to civilization itself.

I am not so sure. Family dinners in my house were commonly unhappy and occasionally violent affairs (Lady Caroline was wrong, by the way, about dinner and relatives), but lunch was different. Lunch was a promise of good things to come, good things wrapped like holiday presents in shiny foil. It might be baloney, peanut butter, ham, tuna, turkey, or cheese. Whatever the sandwich, always lunch meant freedom. Lunch was liberation from the classroom and the tedium of schoolwork.

Whether it is lunch or dinner whose passing we should bewail, it is true that much depends on dinner and on lunch, too. If the demise of both is partly because no one has the time for either, then omelets can help. Omelets make a fine meal at any time, in part because they pair so well with so many different kinds of foods. Not so much for lunch, you may be thinking, at least not during the week, when few if any of us have time or kitchen in which to play. But as you'll see in this chapter, omelets make great sandwiches.

Among my favorite luncheon and dinner omelets are seafood omelets and vegetable omelets. Seafood omelets, for some reason I do not fully understand, seem to be somewhat uncommon now in American restaurants and even more so in home kitchens. They are surprisingly simple to prepare and can be as elegant or as unassuming as one desires. Vegetable omelets are good for us in a way nutritionists and doctors cannot comprehend—they remind us that we, too, are of the good earth, and in so doing vegetables nourish soma and spirit.

In this chapter, I offer a variety of recipes especially well suited to brunch with friends, a light lunch, or a casual supper. I have also included a few stately enough to serve at a fine dinner. Many of these recipes also work well as appetizers and finger foods.

Omelet with Lobster, Shrimp, Truffles, and Tomatoes

Omelette dieppoise

No omelet is more satiny, more elegant, more the embodiment of haute cuisine and fine dining than an Omelette dieppoise. In French cuisine, *dieppoise* refers to the city of Dieppe, in Normandy, well known for its fish. Consequently, many recipes for an Omelette dieppoise call for mussels and mushrooms, and some for oysters. Mine, however, borrows substantially from Narcissa Chamberlain's version. It is composed of lobster, truffle, cream, shrimp, and tomato sauce. It is an omelet you must sit down to in your dress clothes (or in your pajamas). Do make the lobster-shrimp butter—it pairs well with all sorts of dishes, not just omelets!

Serves 1
Master Technique: French/Rolled

⅓ cup lobster meat, cooked and sliced (save the shell for the lobster-shrimp butter)
¼ cup (4 to 6 ounces) medium shrimp, cooked (save the shells for the lobster-shrimp butter)
1 truffle, chopped
2 tablespoons unsalted butter
Salt and freshly ground black pepper
⅛ teaspoon cayenne pepper
¼ cup heavy cream
1 teaspoon Lobster-Shrimp Butter (recipe follows)
3 eggs, mixed
1 tablespoon white wine
1 ½ teaspoons finely chopped fresh flat-leaf parsley, plus more for garnish
½ cup Tomato Concassée (page 000)

Warm the cooked lobster and the truffle in 1 tablespoon of the butter in a small pan over low heat, add salt and pepper to taste, and the cayenne. Add the heavy cream and lobster-shrimp butter and stir gently to incorporate.

Remove the lobster meat, set aside and keep warm. Reduce the cream until it thickens to 2 to 3 tablespoons.

Preheat a nonstick, 8- or 9-inch skillet over medium to medium-high heat.

Whisk the eggs, wine, parsley, salt, and pepper with a fork until just combined. Stop when the eggs just begin to foam, about 15 to 20 seconds.

Melt the remaining tablespoon of butter in the skillet, swirl to coat the pan, and when the butter bubbles and sizzles, pour the eggs into the pan.

Let the eggs sit undisturbed for about 5 seconds. With a fork or a spatula, move the eggs in a circular pattern, moving the eggs from the outside of the pan to the inside. At the same time, using sharp, short, and controlled motions, keep the skillet moving back and forth.

Spoon the lobster over the center of the eggs.

Remove the pan from the heat and use a fork to "roll" the eggs from the far side of the pan to the side closest to you. Do not let the eggs brown or stiffen.

Grab underneath the handle of the pan with the palm of your hand, thumb on top of the handle, and invert the omelet, seam side down, onto the plate.

Spoon the reduced cream sauce over the omelet.

Dress the omelet with the shrimp and tomato concassée. Garnish with parsley.

- -

Variations: Crab or scallops make excellent substitutions for the lobster.

- -

A TIP FROM MY MOTHER: This omelet would make a fine dinner for a prom date.

recipe continues . . .

Lobster-Shrimp Butter

2 to 3 tablespoons coarsely crushed lobster shells and shrimp shells
1 tablespoon unsalted butter
1 teaspoon chopped fresh flat-leaf parsley

Prepare a double boiler over simmering water.

Put the shells, butter, and a couple of drops of water in the top of the double boiler. Simmer for about 15 minutes.

Pour the butter slowly through a fine-mesh strainer into a bowl. If there is butter still in or on the shells, pour a tablespoon or two of very hot water over the shells into the same bowl.

Add the parsley and chill the lobster-shrimp butter.

Puree of Asparagus
and White Wine Omelet

Asparagus is a familiar ingredient in omelets the world over. This very old recipe is a little unusual in calling for the asparagus to be pureed and folded into the omelet. It is based on a Roman recipe called Aliter Patina de Asparagis, from one of the world's first cookbooks, Marcus Gavius Apicius's *De Re Coquinaria* (The Art of Cooking), published in the late fourth or early fifth century.

....

SERVES 1
Master Technique: American/Folded

½ cup Puree of Asparagus (recipe follows)
2 tablespoons grated Parmigiano-Reggiano
1 tablespoon heavy cream
White wine or chicken stock, for thinning (optional)
Salt and fresh ground black pepper
2 eggs, mixed
1 tablespoon white wine
1 tablespoon unsalted butter
Asparagus tips for garnish
Finely diced red bell pepper for garnish
Finely chopped chives for garnish

Combine the puree of asparagus with the grated cheese and heavy cream. The puree should be about the consistency of a thick sauce. If necessary, thin the puree with a little white wine or chicken stock. Season with salt and black pepper.

Preheat a nonstick 8- or 9-inch skillet over medium to medium-high heat.

recipe continues...

Whisk the eggs, 2 tablespoons of the asparagus mixture, wine, salt, and black pepper with a fork until just combined. Stop when the eggs just begin to foam, about 15 to 20 seconds.

Melt the butter in the skillet, swirl to coat the pan, and when the butter sizzles, add the eggs. Swirl the eggs so they cover the entire bottom of the pan. Let the eggs sit quietly for about 10 seconds.

Holding the handle of the pan and using a spatula, pull the uncooked egg toward the center of the pan, proceeding calmly and deliberately around the compass, north to south to east to west. Use a spatula to lift the eggs from the rim of the pan, and move the remaining uncooked egg under the cooked portion.

Let the omelet cook for a minute or two, occasionally moving the uncooked egg under the cooked portion as necessary.

Using a spatula, fold the omelet in half, moving from the outside of the pan to the inside.

Grab underneath the handle of the pan with the palm of your hand, thumb on top of the handle, and turn out the omelet onto a warm plate.

Spoon the remaining puree around the omelet. Garnish with asparagus tips and very finely diced red bell peppers or finely chopped chives.

Variations: I love this recipe with pureed string beans, but a puree of almost any green vegetable will work equally well. Or try a puree of carrot (page 000). You might also consider folding 2 tablespoons of the puree of asparagus directly into the mixed eggs before putting the eggs into the pan. The asparagus colors the eggs beautifully.

Puree of Asparagus

1 tablespoon olive oil
1 medium shallot, chopped
1 small bunch thin asparagus (about 12), thinly sliced
¼ cup chicken stock
Salt and freshly ground black pepper
1 teaspoon fresh lemon juice

Fill a kettle with water and bring to a boil.

Prepare an ice water bath.

Sauté the shallot in the olive oil in a large saucepan over medium-low heat. Add the asparagus and cook for about 1 minute. Do not let the asparagus brown.

Add boiling water to cover asparagus and let cook until the asparagus is tender (3 to 4 minutes, depending on how thick the asparagus is).

Remove the asparagus and place in the ice water bath. When the asparagus has cooled, transfer to a blender and puree, adding chicken stock as necessary. (We want a fairly thick puree.) Season with salt and pepper and lemon juice.

Omelet with Swiss Chard and Caramelized Onions

Swiss chard is one of my favorite greens, but only when I am sure it is fresh. It gets bitter with old age, but when it is young, it is quite sweet, unusual among greens. If you think your Swiss chard might be a bit mature, invigorate it with a soak in a warm bath of chicken broth and garlic.

....

SERVES 2 TO 3
Master Technique: Flat Omelet

¼ cup yellow onion, sliced thinly lengthwise
2 tablespoons unsalted butter
2 tablespoons olive oil
1 teaspoon sugar
Salt and freshly ground black pepper
3 to 4 cups sliced Swiss chard
6 eggs, mixed
2 tablespoons white wine

Caramelize the sliced onion in the 1 tablespoon of the butter, 1 teaspoon of the olive oil, and sugar in a skillet over medium-low heat until golden brown, 15 or 20 minutes. Season with salt and pepper and set aside.

Preheat the broiler.

Rinse the chard (it can be gritty or sandy) and pat dry.

Fold the chard in half along the red stem. Remove the leafy greens from the stem.

Layer the chard leaves and roll tightly lengthwise. Slice in a rough chiffonade.

Preheat a nonstick, ovenproof 10- or 12-inch skillet (a seasoned cast-iron skillet is also a good choice) over medium to medium-low heat.

Sauté the chard in 2 teaspoons of the olive oil until the chard just wilts. Season with salt and pepper.

Whisk the eggs, caramelized onion, wine, salt, and pepper with a fork until just combined.

Heat the remaining 1 tablespoon of the olive oil, swirl to coat the pan, and when it shimmers, add the eggs to the chard. Cook over low heat until the eggs set, approximately 5 to 6 minutes. If there is uncooked egg, lift an edge up and tilt the pan so the uncooked egg runs underneath the cooked egg.

Place the omelet under the broiler until the eggs are puffy and slightly brown, perhaps 1 to 2 minutes. Slide onto a plate and garnish. If you prefer, you can invert the omelet onto the plate.

Variations: You can substitute almost any leafy green for the Swiss chard with excellent results. Chard also pairs well with tomatoes and cheeses.

Steak and Eggs Omelet

Okay, the name is a little redundant. But I like the way it sounds, and it reminds me of a long-gone restaurant chain known as Steak N' Egg. They were tiny, dreary little places, open 24 hours, perfect for breakfast just after last call, when we were very hungry, very broke, and not very fussy. Almost any kind of beef or steak will work in this recipe. An omelet at 3:00 a.m. on the weekend demands a sirloin and hash browns. (My memories of the old Steak N' Egg restaurants are fuddled, but I'm pretty sure every meal came with hash browns.) Valentine's Day calls for a petite fillet and potatoes dauphinoise. I like to garnish this omelet with a quick sauté of red and green bell peppers and onions. This recipe also shouts for a sauce, and almost any will do, including ketchup, a bottled steak sauce, or Worcestershire. For something a little more unusual, however, use flank or skirt steak and pair it with a peppery chimichurri!

....

Serves 1

Master Technique: American/Folded

1 tablespoon olive oil
2 tablespoons chopped green bell pepper
2 tablespoons chopped red bell pepper
2 tablespoons chopped yellow onion
Salt and freshly ground black pepper
3 eggs, mixed
1 tablespoon water
2 or 3 drops Tabasco
1 tablespoon unsalted butter
4 to 6 ounces steak, cooked and sliced thinly, kept warm

Preheat a nonstick, 8- or 9-inch skillet over medium to medium-high heat.

Sauté the peppers and onions in olive oil until just tender. Season with salt and pepper. Set aside and keep warm.

Preheat a nonstick, 8- or 9-inch skillet over medium to medium-high heat.

Whisk the eggs, water, Tabasco, salt, and black pepper with a fork until just combined. Stop when the eggs just begin to foam, about 15 to 20 seconds.

Melt the butter in the skillet, swirl to coat the pan, and when the butter sizzles, add the eggs. Swirl the eggs so they cover the entire bottom of the pan. Let the eggs sit quietly for about 10 seconds.

Holding the handle of the pan and using a spatula, pull the uncooked egg toward the center of the pan, proceeding calmly and deliberately around the compass, north to south to east to west. Use a spatula to lift the eggs from the rim of the pan, and move the remaining uncooked egg under the cooked portion.

Let the omelet cook for a minute or two, occasionally moving the uncooked egg under the cooked portion as necessary.

Add half of the sliced steak to the center of the omelet.

Using a spatula, fold the omelet in half, moving from the outside of the pan to the inside.

Grab underneath the handle of the pan with the palm of your hand, thumb on top of the handle, and turn out the omelet onto a warm plate.

Surround and cover the omelet with the remaining steak and the sauté of bell pepper and onion.

Variation: I give you, in all seriousness, the Chicken-Fried Steak Omelet (recipe follows).

Chicken-Fried Steak Omelet

I think I am prouder of this omelet than any other in this little book! Indeed, this is one of those times where the variation is far superior to the original. Serve with a biscuit and butter.

....

SERVES 1
Master Technique: American/Folded

3 eggs, mixed
1 tablespoon chicken stock or water
2 or 3 drops Tabasco
Salt and freshly ground black pepper
1 tablespoon unsalted butter
6 ounces Chicken-Fried Steak (recipe follows), kept warm
Black Pepper Gravy (recipe follows)

Preheat a nonstick, 8- or 9-inch skillet over medium to medium-high heat.

Whisk the eggs, chicken stock, Tabasco, salt, and pepper with a fork until just combined.

Melt the butter in the skillet, swirl to coat the pan, and when the butter sizzles, add the eggs. Swirl the eggs so they cover the entire bottom of the pan. Let the eggs sit quietly for about 10 seconds.

Holding the handle of the pan and using a spatula, pull the uncooked egg toward the center of the pan, proceeding calmly and deliberately around the compass, north to south to east to west. Use a spatula to lift the eggs from the rim of the pan, and move the remaining uncooked egg under the cooked portion.

Let the omelet cook for a minute or two, occasionally moving the uncooked egg under the cooked portion as necessary.

Using a spatula, fold the omelet in half, moving from the outside of the pan to the inside.

Place the chicken-fried steak on a warm plate.

Grab underneath the handle of the pan with the palm of your hand, thumb on top of the handle, and invert the omelet, seam side down, onto the steak.

Surround and cover the omelet with the black pepper gravy.

Chicken-Fried Steak

I hope you already have a favorite recipe for chicken-fried steak. If not, then please try this one, but be aware that opinions about how to prepare chicken-fried steak, like opinions about chili, cheesesteaks, and politics, are the stuff of madness.

6 to 8 ounces thin round or beefsteak or cube steak
Salt and freshly ground black pepper
½ cup all-purpose flour, for dredging
2 eggs
1 tablespoon milk
2 or 3 drops Tabasco
2 tablespoons vegetable oil or lard
1 teaspoon unsalted butter

Pound and tenderize the steaks with a mallet until the meat is very thin (about ⅛ inch).

Season the steaks with salt and a generous amount of black pepper.

On a plate, combine the flour with 1 tablespoon of black pepper (more, if desired) and 1 teaspoon of salt.

In a shallow bowl, mix the eggs, milk, and Tabasco to make an egg wash.

Dredge the steaks in the flour mixture and shake off the excess flour.

Dip the steaks in the wash.

Dredge the steaks a second time in the flour mixture and leave to sit about 10 minutes. This helps the flour to adhere to the meat.

Heat the oil and butter in a large skillet over medium heat.

recipe continues . . .

When the oil shimmers, add the steaks to the pan, taking care not to crowd them. Cook until deep brown, 4 to 5 minutes, and then flip and cook for an additional 3 to 4 minutes. Remove from the heat and keep warm.

Drain the oil, leaving about 3 tablespoons in the pan to make the gravy.

Black Pepper Gravy

What is the difference between a sauce and a gravy? Some folks say a gravy starts with a roux, using the juices that come from cooking meat or poultry and whisking them with flour, whereas a sauce can be conjured out of most anything. To my mind, a black pepper gravy is a white sauce with an appetite for life.

3 tablespoons oil or butter (reserved from Chicken-Fried Steak pan)
3 tablespoons all-purpose flour
1 cup whole milk
⅛ teaspoon cayenne pepper
Whole milk or chicken stock, for thinning (optional)
Salt and freshly ground black pepper

Heat the oil in a 10- or 12-inch skillet over medium heat.

Add the flour to the butter to make a roux. Stir the flour with a wooden spoon or spatula and cook until the flour looks sandy, about 2 minutes.

Slowly add ½ cup of the milk and cayenne and whisk vigorously to incorporate the flour. After a minute or two, add another ½ cup of the milk and cook until the sauce thickens, about 5 minutes. If the gravy is too thick, thin with a little milk or chicken stock. Season with salt and a generous amount of black pepper.

Omelet with Crawfish

Omelette nantua

Traditionally a dish styled *nantua* includes crawfish or crawfish tails, and a sauce nantua uses a crawfish stock or reduction as one of its essential ingredients. I was somewhat surprised, therefore, to encounter recipes for "omelets nantua" that use shrimp or even chicken. But a quick check of Escoffier finds that small shrimp are an acceptable substitute for the crawfish, and the whole point of *The Perfect Omelet* is to play. If you can't find crawfish at the fishmonger near you, try the shrimp.

....

SERVES 1

Master Technique: American/Folded

2 eggs, mixed
1 tablespoon white wine or vinegar
Salt and freshly ground black pepper
1 tablespoon unsalted butter
¼ cup cooked crawfish meat, chopped, or small shrimp, plus 1 or 2 cooked whole
    small crawfish, crawfish tails, or shrimp for garnish
1 recipe Sauce Nantua (recipe follows)
Chopped scallions or parsley for garnish

Preheat a nonstick, 8- or 9-inch skillet over medium to medium-high heat.

Whisk the eggs, wine, salt, and pepper with a fork until just combined.

Melt the butter in the skillet, swirl to coat the pan, and when the butter sizzles, add the eggs. Swirl the eggs so they cover the entire bottom of the pan. Let the eggs sit quietly for about 10 seconds.

Holding the handle of the pan and using a spatula, pull the uncooked egg toward the center of the pan, proceeding calmly and deliberately around the compass, north to south to east to west. Use a spatula to lift the eggs from the rim of the pan, and move the remaining uncooked egg under the cooked portion.

recipe continues . . .

Let the omelet cook for a minute or two, occasionally moving the uncooked egg under the cooked portion as necessary.

Add the crawfish to the center of the eggs.

Using a spatula, fold the omelet in half, moving from the outside of the pan to the inside.

Grab underneath the handle of the pan with the palm of your hand, thumb on top of the handle, and turn out the omelet onto a warm plate, coated with ¼ cup of the sauce nantua.

Spoon 2 tablespoons of the sauce over the top of the omelet. Place one or two small crawfish tails (or small shrimp) on top and garnish with chopped scallions or parsley.

Variation: Narcissa Chamberlain includes a recipe for a Chicken Omelet Nantua in her classic book of omelets. Her version calls for six eggs; ¾ cup of diced, cooked chicken meat; ½ truffle, sliced and cooked in butter; and a little chicken stock. She serves the omelet with ¼ cup of sauce nantua spooned over the top of the omelet.

A TIP FROM MY MOTHER: A good fish stock should be a staple in your kitchen. Shrimp and lobster shells freeze well. Store them in freezer bags whenever you make shrimp, and take them out to make a quick stock as needed.

Sauce Nantua

This recipe departs a bit from the original, but it has the traditional béchamel base flavored with stock and butter. It is versatile and pairs well with most seafood and chicken omelets.

1 tablespoon unsalted butter
1 tablespoon all-purpose flour
1 ½ teaspoons tomato paste
1 tablespoon fish stock (use the shrimp shells, but clam juice, chicken stock, or vegetable stock are good substitutes), plus more if needed
½ cup light cream
Salt and freshly ground black pepper
½ teaspoon cayenne pepper

Combine the butter and flour in a 10-inch skillet to make a roux. Cook for about 2 minutes, until sandy in color, to remove the taste of the raw flour.

Add the tomato paste, fish stock, and 3 tablespoons of the cream. Mix vigorously and cook over medium-low heat. As the mixture begins to thicken, add the remaining 5 tablespoons of cream, salt, and pepper. Cook until the sauce thickens and then remove from the heat. Add the cayenne. Keep warm and adjust the seasoning.

If the sauce is too thick, thin it with additional stock.

Cold Omelet Sandwich with Frisée and Caramelized Onions

My mother was weird, as I think you have probably already surmised. Other kids opened their lunch boxes to find sandwiches wrapped in neat plastic bags that folded cleanly or, in some cases, actually had zippers. My mother, however, wrapped our lunches—sandwiches, too—in tinfoil, presumably to humiliate us in front of the other kids. Eventually I came to like it (the foil, not the humiliation). Who knew what was inside my carefully gift-wrapped present? Sadly, there was never an omelet sandwich. . . . This recipe uses 2 eggs, but I often make omelets for sandwiches with only 1 egg, which keeps the omelet thinner and makes it a little easier to layer between the bread.

....

SERVES 1 TO 2
Technique: American/Folded

½ cup sliced yellow onion
1 tablespoon plus 1 teaspoon unsalted butter
1 teaspoon olive oil
Salt and freshly ground black pepper
2 eggs, mixed
1 tablespoon water
2 slices good bread, or 1 crusty roll, sliced
2 or 3 leaves frisée or similar green
Olive oil or balsamic vinegar, to dress

Sauté the onion in 1 teaspoon of the butter and the oil over low heat until golden brown, 15 to 20 minutes, season with salt and pepper, and set aside.

Preheat a nonstick, 8- or 9-inch skillet over medium to medium-high heat.

Whisk the eggs, water, salt, and pepper with a fork until just combined.

Melt the remaining 1 tablespoon butter in the skillet, swirl to coat the pan, and when the butter sizzles, add the eggs. Swirl the eggs so they cover the entire bottom of the pan. Let the eggs sit quietly for about 10 seconds.

Holding the handle of the pan and using a spatula, pull the uncooked egg toward the center of the pan, proceeding calmly and deliberately around the compass, north to south to east to west. Use a spatula to lift the eggs from the rim of the pan, and move the remaining uncooked egg under the cooked portion.

Let the omelet cook for a minute or two, occasionally moving the uncooked egg under the cooked portion as necessary.

Add the caramelized onion to the center of the eggs.

Using a spatula, fold the omelet in half, moving from the outside of the pan to the inside.

Grab underneath the handle of the pan with the palm of your hand, thumb on top of the handle, and turn out the omelet onto your bread or roll of choice with a couple of leaves of frisée. I like a good, crusty, peasant bread, or a tart sourdough. Dress with a drizzle of olive oil or balsamic vinegar.

Variations: Cheese goes very well with this omelet (especially Gruyère, or a milder goat cheese). Pretty much any flat omelet makes a fine sandwich, but western sandwiches seem especially common on diner menus, and although ordinarily they are served hot, cold westerns are good, too. For a hot sandwich, try a plain omelet with bacon or ham and tomato.

> **A TIP FROM MY MOTHER:** If you're packing this for school or work, wrap it tightly in tinfoil. Why? Because I said so.

Cold Omelet Sandwich with Bacon and Chives

Some bygone recipes call this omelet a "Savoy," but I have not able to trace the name. Perhaps it has some connection to the Savoy Hotel in London, where Escoffier was chef for many years, but oddly, no such omelet appears in Escoffier's classic cookbook. Maybe its origins reach as far back as the House of Savoy in 15th-century Italy. In both cases, the term connotes royalty. So, lunch like a prince or a princess, or an earl . . . of Sandwich.

....

SERVES 1
Master Technique: American/Folded

2 eggs, mixed
1 tablespoon water
Salt and freshly ground black pepper
1 tablespoon unsalted butter
2 to 4 slices bacon, cooked and chopped (about ⅓ cup)
2 tablespoons finely chopped fresh chives
2 slices good bread, or 1 crusty roll, sliced
Chives or chive blossoms for garnish

Preheat a nonstick, 8- or 9-inch skillet over medium to medium-high heat.

Whisk the eggs, water, salt, and pepper with a fork until just combined.

Melt the butter in the skillet, swirl to coat the pan, and when the butter sizzles, add the eggs. Swirl the eggs so they cover the entire bottom of the pan. Let the eggs sit quietly for about 10 seconds.

Holding the handle of the pan and using a spatula, pull the uncooked egg toward the center of the pan, proceeding calmly and deliberately around the compass, north to south to east to west. Use a spatula to lift the eggs from the rim of the pan, and move the remaining uncooked egg under the cooked portion.

Let the omelet cook for a minute or two, occasionally moving the uncooked egg under the cooked portion as necessary.

Add the bacon and chives to the center of the eggs.

Using a spatula, fold the omelet in half, moving from the outside of the pan to the inside.

Grab underneath the handle of the pan with the palm of your hand, thumb on top of the handle, and turn out the omelet onto your bread or roll. Garnish with whole chives or chive blossoms.

Omelet with Bell Peppers and Onion

Omelette piperade

A piperade is a sauté of onions, bell peppers, and tomatoes. This omelet is from the Basque regions of France (*piperade*) and Spain (*piperrada*). It was one of the first omelets I learned in culinary school; it is still one of my favorites. A single slice makes a great sandwich.

....

SERVES 3 TO 4
Master Technique: Flat

1 tablespoon olive oil
¼ cup sliced red bell pepper
¼ cup sliced green bell pepper
¼ cup thinly sliced white onion
Salt and freshly ground black pepper
¼ cup chopped plum tomato
1 garlic clove, minced
1 teaspoon smoked paprika
½ teaspoon ground cumin
6 eggs, mixed
2 tablespoons water or white wine
1 tablespoon unsalted butter (optional)
2 tablespoons grated Spanish cheese, such as Idiazabal (optional)
1 tablespoon chopped fresh flat-leaf parsley for garnish

Preheat the broiler.

Preheat a nonstick, ovenproof 10- or 12-inch skillet (a seasoned cast-iron skillet is also a good choice) over medium to medium-low heat.

Lightly sauté the peppers and onion with salt and black pepper in the olive oil. When the peppers are soft and the onion translucent or golden, add the tomato, garlic, paprika, and cumin, and sauté for about another minute. Do not let the garlic burn.

Whisk the eggs, water, salt, and pepper with a fork until just combined.

Add 1 tablespoon of butter to the pan, if necessary. Add the egg mixture to the mixture in the skillet.

Cook over low heat until the eggs set, approximately 5 to 6 minutes. If there is uncooked egg, lift an edge up and tilt the pan so the uncooked egg runs underneath the cooked egg.

Place the omelet under the broiler until the eggs finish cooking and are slightly brown; this should take no more than a minute or two. Garnish with grated cheese and chopped parsley.

Variation: A nice Spanish ham, such as a Bayonne, a Serrano or, if you can splurge, a *jamón ibérico*, is the perfect (whatever that means) addition to this omelet.

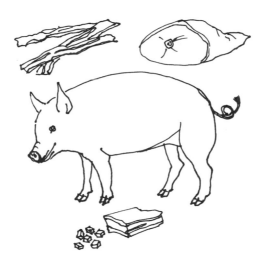

Omelet with Mussels, Tomatoes, and Garlic with White Wine

Mussels make for an uncommon but delicious omelet. This recipe calls for chopped tomatoes in the eggs and for garnish. I like to double the tomatoes and use the extra as a sauce to surround the eggs, which of course requires the company of a good crusty bread, which in turn demands a dry white wine.

....

Serves 1
Master Technique: American/Folded

¼ cup white wine
1 tablespoon plus 1 teaspoon finely chopped fresh flat-leaf parsley
1 garlic clove, left whole, plus 1 clove chopped
½ small lemon
½ pound small mussels, with shells, cleaned and bearded
Salt and freshly ground black pepper
½ cup chopped plum tomato
2 eggs, mixed
1 tablespoon unsalted butter

Fill a steamer pot with water and the white wine, the teaspoon of chopped parsley, the whole garlic clove, and the lemon half, and steam the mussels over the mixture.

When the shells open, remove the mussels and drain them, reserving 2 tablespoons of the steaming liquid (mussel juice). Chop the mussels if large, season with salt and pepper, and set aside. Save a few shells for garnish.

Season the chopped tomato with salt and pepper, drain, and set aside.

Preheat a nonstick, 8- or 9-inch skillet over medium to medium-high heat.

Whisk the eggs, 1 tablespoon of mussel juice, salt, and pepper with a fork until just combined.

Melt the butter in the skillet, swirl to coat the pan, and when the butter sizzles, add the eggs. Swirl the eggs so they cover the entire bottom of the pan. Let the eggs sit quietly for about 10 seconds.

Holding the handle of the pan and using a spatula, pull the uncooked egg toward the center of the pan, proceeding calmly and deliberately around the compass, north to south to east to west. Use a spatula to lift the eggs from the rim of the pan, and move the remaining uncooked egg under the cooked portion.

Let the omelet cook for a minute or two, occasionally moving the uncooked egg under the cooked portion as necessary.

Add the mussels, tomato, and chopped garlic, reserving 1 to 2 tablespoons of the tomato for garnish.

Using a spatula, fold the omelet in half, moving from the outside of the pan to the inside.

Grab underneath the handle of the pan with the palm of your hand, thumb on top of the handle, and turn out the omelet onto a warm plate.

Garnish with the tomatoes and sprinkle with the reserved parsley. Decorate the plate with a few mussel shells.

Variation: One word: spinach!

Carrot Omelet

If you think the only good carrot is in a cake, then this omelet will be quite a treat. I am at a loss to explain why carrots are the object of so much derision. It seems we eat them raw, especially when we are dieting, or we boil them until they are shapeless and tasteless. This omelet celebrates the carrot by using a well-seasoned puree of carrot to give the eggs a rich, burnt ocher color.

....

SERVES 1

Master Technique: American/Folded

2 eggs, mixed
1 tablespoon white wine
¼ cup plus 2 tablespoons Puree of Carrot (recipe follows) (save greens for garnish)
Salt and freshly ground black pepper
1 tablespoon unsalted butter
1 tablespoon finely chopped fresh flat-leaf parsley for garnish

Preheat a nonstick, 8- or 9-inch skillet over medium to medium-high heat.

Whisk the eggs, wine, 2 tablespoons of the carrot puree, and salt and pepper with a fork until just combined.

Melt the butter in the skillet, swirl to coat the pan, and when the butter sizzles, add the eggs. Swirl the eggs so they cover the entire bottom of the pan. Let the eggs sit quietly for about 10 seconds.

Holding the handle of the pan and using a spatula, pull the uncooked egg toward the center of the pan, proceeding calmly and deliberately around the compass, north to south to east to west. Use a spatula to lift the eggs from the rim of the pan, and move the remaining uncooked egg under the cooked portion.

Let the omelet cook for a minute or two, occasionally moving the uncooked egg under the cooked portion as necessary.

Spread the remaining ¼ cup of carrot puree over the center of the eggs.

Using a spatula, fold the omelet in half, moving from the outside of the pan to the inside.

Grab underneath the handle of the pan with the palm of your hand, thumb on top of the handle, and turn out the omelet onto a warm plate.

Garnish with chopped parsley or, if you have them, the carrot greens.

Puree of Carrot

This puree makes a wonderful side dish for almost any meal and the basic method works well with asparagus, string beans, celeriac, and most other root vegetables. It is important to season the carrots thoroughly. Like potatoes, carrots marry well with salt, pepper, and butter. Many recipes ask the cook to boil the carrots until they are very tender, but I prefer to roast them in the oven with a little olive oil.

. . . .

3 to 4 (about ½ pound) medium carrots (save the greens)
Olive oil, for roasting
Salt and freshly ground black pepper
1 teaspoon sugar (optional)
¼ cup chicken stock
1 tablespoon unsalted butter
1 teaspoon fresh lemon juice (optional)

Preheat the oven to 425°F

Remove and set aside the green tops. Peel the carrots. If the carrots are large, cut them in half.

Roast the carrots, dressed in olive oil, salt, and pepper, on a thin baking sheet until they begin to turn deep brown and tender, about 20 minutes. Add the sugar at the start of the roasting, if you think your carrots are not sweet.

Put the carrots in a bowl, add 2 tablespoons of the chicken stock, salt and pepper, and butter, and mash until there are no lumps. If the puree is too thick, add additional stock, but you do want a fairly thick consistency. You can also puree the carrots in a food processor.

Adjust the seasonings. If you want to store the puree in the refrigerator, add 1 teaspoon of lemon juice.

Curried Salmon and Carrot Omelet

This is one of my go-to omelets when I want to impress.

....

SERVES 1

Master Technique: American/Folded

½ cup Puree of Carrot (page 000)

2 to 4 teaspoons curry powder (substitute 1 teaspoon ground cumin or ginger for the first teaspoon, if desired)

One 4- to 5-ounce salmon fillet

Salt and freshly ground black pepper

2 tablespoons plain nonfat Greek yogurt

½ teaspoon ground cumin

⅛ teaspoon ground ginger

½ teaspoon fresh lemon juice

2 eggs, mixed

1 tablespoon white wine

1 tablespoon unsalted butter

1 tablespoon finely chopped fresh flat-leaf parsley

Chopped scallions for garnish

Carrot greens for garnish (optional)

Preheat the oven to 425°F.

Add 1 teaspoon of the curry powder (or of ground cumin or ginger) to the carrot puree.

Place the salmon fillet on a piece of foil on a baking sheet. Season the fillet with the remaining 1 to 3 teaspoons of curry powder, salt, and pepper, and roast until the fish just begins to flake and is pink inside—about 10 minutes. Allow the salmon to cool, then flake into large chunks. Discard the skin.

Combine the yogurt, cumin, ginger, and lemon juice in a small bowl and set aside.

Preheat a nonstick, 8- or 9-inch skillet over medium to medium-high heat.

Whisk the eggs, wine, salt, and pepper with a fork until just combined.

Melt the butter in the skillet, swirl to coat the pan, and when the butter sizzles, add the eggs. Swirl the eggs so they cover the entire bottom of the pan. Let the eggs sit quietly for about 10 seconds.

Holding the handle of the pan and using a spatula, pull the uncooked egg toward the center of the pan, proceeding calmly and deliberately around the compass, north to south to east to west. Use a spatula to lift the eggs from the rim of the pan, and move the remaining uncooked egg under the cooked portion.

Let the omelet cook for a minute or two, occasionally moving the uncooked egg under the cooked portion as necessary.

Spread the carrot puree over the center of the eggs and then top with the flaked salmon.

Using a spatula, fold the omelet in half, moving from the outside of the pan to the inside.

Grab underneath the handle of the pan with the palm of your hand, thumb on top of the handle, and turn out the omelet onto a warm plate. Spoon the yogurt sauce over the omelet.

Garnish with chopped scallions or, if you have them, the carrot greens.

Mustard and Mustard Greens Omelet

This unusual omelet is well worth the trouble of securing fresh mustard greens. Look for them early in the spring. (You can also find frozen mustard greens in some grocery stores, but I don't care for them.) Wash the mustard greens thoroughly before you use them. Like leeks, they attract sand and soil.

....

SERVES 1

Master Technique: French/Rolled

½ cup (about 1 ounce) very small croutons or coarse bread crumbs

2 tablespoons unsalted butter

Salt and freshly ground black pepper

1 bunch fresh mustard greens, washed and chopped into ½-inch pieces (about 1 cup)

1 teaspoon olive oil

1 teaspoon red wine vinegar

2 eggs, mixed

1 tablespoon coarse Dijon mustard

1 tablespoon finely chopped fresh flat-leaf parsley for garnish

---

Toast croutons in 1 tablespoon of the butter melted in a skillet over medium heat. Season with salt and pepper and set aside.

Preheat a nonstick, 8- or 9-inch skillet over medium heat.

Sauté the mustard greens in the olive oil until just wilted. They cook very quickly. Set aside and season with the red wine vinegar, salt, and pepper. You should have about ½ cup of cooked greens.

Preheat a nonstick, 8- or 9-inch skillet over medium to medium-high heat.

Whisk the eggs, half of the mustard greens, salt, and pepper with a fork until just combined.

Melt the butter in the skillet, swirl to coat the pan, and when the butter bubbles and sizzles, pour the eggs into the pan.

Let the eggs sit undisturbed for about 5 seconds. With a fork or a spatula, move the eggs in a circular pattern, moving the eggs from the outside of the pan to the inside. At the same time, using sharp, short, and controlled motions, keep the skillet moving back and forth.

Spoon the remaining mustard greens and half of the croutons over the center of the omelet.

After the eggs have begun to form curds, but before they stiffen completely, perhaps 10 seconds, remove the pan from the heat and use the fork to "roll" the eggs from the far side of the pan to the side closest to you. Do not let the eggs brown or stiffen.

Grab underneath the handle of the pan with the palm of your hand, thumb on top of the handle, and invert the omelet, seam side down, onto the plate.

Dress the omelet with parsley or additional mustard greens and the remaining croutons.

Variation: This recipe also makes a very nice small frittata.

Omelet with Poached Chicken

Omelette Pierre Franey

For too brief a time, just before he passed away, the great French chef Pierre Franey was an adviser to my class at culinary school. Franey, executive chef at Le Pavillon in New York City, was admired for his iconic cookbooks, *The 60-Minute Gourmet* and *More 60-Minute Gourmet*, both of which are full of wisdom and good humor. He was also a friend. I don't know if he'd want to have an omelet in his tribute (given his first experience at the restaurant Drouant, maybe he'd appreciate the irony), but I do think he would like this simple omelet, modeled on the very first omelet recipe to make an appearance in *The 60-Minute Gourmet*. I think this omelet is a little easier to make if you use the American/Folded Master Technique, but Franey was French, so I had little choice in the matter. Franey proposed asparagus with a compound nutmeg butter to accompany his Omelette à la Reine. It's an excellent suggestion.

....

SERVES 1
Master Technique: French/Rolled

3 eggs, mixed
1 tablespoon white wine
Salt and freshly ground black pepper
1 tablespoon unsalted butter, plus a pat for garnish
1 recipe Poulet Poché (recipe follows)
1 tablespoon fresh flat-leaf parsley for garnish

Preheat a nonstick, 8- or 9-inch skillet over medium heat.

Whisk the eggs, wine, salt, and pepper with a fork until just combined.

Melt the butter in the skillet, swirl to coat the pan, and when the butter bubbles and sizzles, pour the eggs into the pan.

Let the eggs sit undisturbed for about 5 seconds. With a fork or a spatula, move the eggs in a circular pattern, moving the eggs from the outside of the pan to the inside.

At the same time, using sharp, short, and controlled motions, keep the skillet moving back and forth.

Spoon about two tablespoons of the shredded chicken breast over the center of the omelet.

Remove the pan from the heat and use the fork to "roll" the eggs from the far side of the pan to the side closest to you. Do not let the eggs brown or stiffen.

Grab underneath the handle of the pan with the palm of your hand, thumb on top of the handle, and invert the omelet, seam side down, onto the plate.

Dress the omelet with a very thin pat of butter and parsley.

Poulet Poché

Poached Chicken

1 small boneless, skinless chicken breast (4 to 6 ounces)
1 cup water
1 tablespoon white wine or Champagne vinegar
1 sprig flat-leaf parsley
1 bay leaf
1 small onion, cut in half, skin on
1 small carrot, cut in half, skin on
4 to 6 whole peppercorns
Salt and freshly ground black pepper

Place all the ingredients in a saucepan and bring to a boil. Lower the heat to a soft simmer, cover, and cook for about 8 minutes, depending upon the weight of the chicken. The chicken should reach an internal temperature of 165°F.

Remove the chicken, allow to cool, shred with a fork, and season with salt and pepper.

Eggplant Omelet

Omelette aubergine

Eggplants are a staple of French cooking and a much favored part of omelet cuisine, not only in France but also, we shall see in the next chapter, in several other cuisines and culinary traditions. This recipe is for a very simple eggplant omelet. Use it as a foundation and add whatever you like! I've made a couple of suggestions below.

SERVES 1

Master Technique: American/Folded

½ cup diced eggplant (about ½-inch dice)
1 teaspoon olive oil
2 eggs, mixed
1 tablespoon white wine or vinegar
Salt and freshly ground black pepper
1 tablespoon unsalted butter
Parsley for garnish

Sauté the diced eggplant until it is tender and soft in the olive oil in a small pan over medium heat, about 4 to 5 minutes. Season well.

Preheat a nonstick, 8- or 9-inch skillet over medium to medium-high heat.

Whisk the eggs, wine, salt, and pepper with a fork until just combined.

Melt the butter in the skillet, swirl to coat the pan, and when the butter sizzles, add the eggs. Swirl the eggs so they cover the entire bottom of the pan. Let the eggs sit quietly for about 10 seconds.

Holding the handle of the pan and using a spatula, pull the uncooked egg toward the center of the pan, proceeding calmly and deliberately around the compass, north to south to east to west. Use a spatula to lift the eggs from the rim of the pan, and move the remaining uncooked egg under the cooked portion.

Let the omelet cook for a minute or two, occasionally moving the uncooked egg under the cooked portion as necessary.

Add the eggplant to the center of the eggs.

Using a spatula, fold the omelet in half, moving from the outside of the pan to the inside.

Grab underneath the handle of the pan with the palm of your hand, thumb on top of the handle, and turn out the omelet onto a warm plate.

Garnish with parsley.

· ·

Variations: An Omelette Aubergine quickly becomes a delicious Omelette Ratatouille with the simple addition of onions, peppers, tomatoes, and a few contributions from your herb garden. Sauté the vegetables until they are soft and tender, spoon a bit of the ratatouille into the center of the omelet before folding it, and spoon the remaining vegetables around and over the top of the plated omelet.

Another very old and traditional omelet with eggplant is an Omelette Mistral. To the sautéed eggplant, add a small chopped tomato, 1 chopped garlic clove, and 1 teaspoon of chopped fresh parsley. The Mistral is usually a flat omelet, but it works just as well with the other techniques.

· ·

Omelet with Beef, Eggplant, Pepper, and Tomato

Omelette Valmy

This is a rich, big omelet, suggesting to me that it honors some great occasion or event. Is it named in honor of the famous Cannonade of Valmy, in which France defeated the Prussians and soon thereafter declared itself for the first time a "republic"? Is it named after the Duc du Valmy, one of the French commanders in that very battle? Maybe this omelet honors the region of Valmy in northeastern France? Perhaps the late French actor, André Valmy? I have no idea. I'm sure you can find something worth celebrating.

....

SERVES 2

Master Technique: American/Folded

2 tablespoons sliced green bell pepper
1 teaspoon olive oil
2 tablespoons diced eggplant
¼ cup plus 2 tablespoons chopped plum tomato, chopped, plus more for garnish
    (or tomato concassée, page 000)
3 to 4 ounces pre-cooked beef steak, sliced
1 garlic clove, minced
4 eggs, mixed
1 tablespoon white wine
Salt and freshly ground black pepper
1 tablespoon unsalted butter
Parsley for garnish

Sauté the bell pepper in olive oil in a small pan over medium heat until it begins to soften.

Add the eggplant and ¼ cup of tomato and cook until tender and soft. Add the steak and garlic, and heat until warm. Season well.

Preheat a nonstick, 8- or 9-inch skillet over medium to medium-high heat.

Whisk the eggs, wine, salt, and black pepper with a fork until just combined.

Melt the butter in the skillet, swirl to coat the pan, and when the butter sizzles, add the eggs. Swirl the eggs so they cover the entire bottom of the pan. Let the eggs sit quietly for about 10 seconds.

Holding the handle of the pan and using a spatula, pull the uncooked egg toward the center of the pan, proceeding calmly and deliberately around the compass, north to south to east to west. Use a spatula to lift the eggs from the rim of the pan, and move the remaining uncooked egg under the cooked portion.

Let the omelet cook for a minute or two, occasionally moving the uncooked egg under the cooked portion as necessary.

Add the steak mixture and remaining 2 tablespoons of tomato to the center of the eggs. Reserve some of the steak for garnish.

Using a spatula, fold the omelet in half, moving from the outside of the pan to the inside.

Grab underneath the handle of the pan with the palm of your hand, thumb on top of the handle, and turn out the omelet onto a warm plate.

Garnish with a few slices of steak and chopped tomato and parsley.

Chapter Four:
International Omelets

〜◦▬◉▬◦〜

Frittatas . . . require only eggs and imagination.

—MICHELLE MAISTO, *THE GASTRONOMY OF MARRIAGE*

One of the finest omelets I have ever known was at the Breakfast Bar at the Holiday Inn in Hefei, China. My wife, my daughter, and I had traveled to China to adopt a little girl. Every morning our group would gather en masse at the breakfast bar on the top floor, infants in arms, sleep deprived and in shock (parents and kids alike). To our left was an improbable variety of Western foods, to the right a traditional Chinese assortment, including (I think) *baozi* (steamed buns), rice and noodles, and, especially for the new adoptees, congee.

The Western front featured an omelet station, manned by a young Chinese chef in starched whites and a towering toque. I speak no Chinese, and he spoke no English, but for several mornings, we had a nice conversation with our hands about omelets. His technique was so pure, so perfect, so . . . well, French, that I wondered where he had learned it.

Although most of us think of omelets as quintessentially French, the origin and reach of the omelet is distinctly global. Most of the world's major cuisines and many of its more obscure ones include egg dishes that evince the French version. Omelets are a rich part of the cuisines of Asia, Arabia, and the Americas, as well of Eastern and Western Europe. The paradigmatic French omelet is no more or less authentic an omelet than an Italian frittata, a Spanish tortilla, a Brazilian *frigideira*, a Persian *kuku*, or a Middle Eastern *eggah* (pronounced "ijja"), which is similar to the frittata and served thick with vegetables. Some scholars have even suggested that the origins of the omelet may trace not to Europe, but to ancient Persia. Observing the likeness between the kuku, the eggah, the tortilla Española, and a North African dish called an *Omelette juive (Jewish omelet)*, Alan Davidson suggests that the tortilla in particular might be a milestone on the omelet trail. The trail runs from Persia to Spain (and, I might hypothesize, to Portugal in the related *tortilha*), helped along by Sephardi Jews "in a number of countries" that made a specialty of potato omelets: "The trail could also have had a branch into Sicily leading to the Italian frittata."

Perhaps. What is the difference, after all, between what the French call a flat or "open-faced" omelet, an Italian frittata, and the Spanish tortilla? An inattentive observer might conclude, for example, that the only significant difference between a frittata and a tortilla is that one is from Italy and one from Spain, although there are some subtle differences (in academic jargon, we call these sorts of subtle variances "fuzzy"), chiefly in the manner of their preparation.

One feature held in common is that all these omelets are prepared typically with the ingredients incorporated into the eggs, and then served open-faced, rather than rolled or folded in the pan. And a flat omelet often uses more eggs, sometimes many more eggs, than a French omelet, although there are exceptions to this rule, as there are to any and all of the rules of omeletry. But the similarities run deep among open-faced omelets.

There are Japanese omelets, such as the *tamagoyaki* (sometimes called a *tamago* roll), consisting of thin layers of rolled eggs, sweet and sometimes seasoned with mirin or soy sauce and prepared in a special square pan called a *makiyakinabe*. Another is the *omurice*, with fried rice and ketchup, popular in parts of South Korea and Taiwan. There are Vietnamese omelets (the French influence is only part of the explanation), Thai omelets, such as *khai yat sai* (very thin, often filled with savory minced meats and fine vegetables and flavored with oyster or fish sauce), and Chinese and Chinese-American omelets, such as egg foo yong. Egg foo yong is a much-traveled dish with as many regional variations as spellings. Is it Egg Fu Yung? Egg Foo Yung? Egg Foyung? I have seen all these and more.

If we relax the definition not very much then, we find that omelets are nearly as ubiquitous (though not as insidious) as the golden arches. (One hates to imagine a McOmelet.) These many variations underscore the philosophy of *The Perfect Omelet*: there is no single, best way to do an omelet. In that spirit, I present a variety of recipes for frittatas, tortillas, eggahs, and kukus, as well as omelets that are Asian, African, and Middle Eastern.

Simple Garlic and Onion Frittata

The trick to this simple and delicious frittata is to be patient with the onions. Let them turn a rich, bricklike brown. They should be very sweet to the taste. Like most of the frittatas in this book, you can cook this one on the stovetop and finish it under the broiler. Cook over low heat until the top of the frittata is nearly set, approximately 10 to 12 minutes (how long will depend on how many eggs you use and the size of your pan), occasionally moving the uncooked egg under the cooked edges. Place the frittata under the broiler until the eggs finish cooking and are slightly browned, just a minute or two.

....

SERVES 4
Master Technique: Flat/Frittata

1 cup thinly sliced onion (about 1 medium)
1 tablespoon unsalted butter
1 tablespoon olive oil, plus 1 to 2 tablespoons more (or butter)
1 teaspoon sugar (optional)
6 garlic cloves, sliced thinly
1 tablespoon sherry or red wine vinegar
Salt and freshly ground black pepper
8 eggs, mixed
½ cup whole milk
1 tablespoon chopped fresh flat-leaf parsley or basil for garnish

---

Preheat the oven to 350°F.

Gently sauté the onion in the butter and the olive oil in an ovenproof 10- or 12-inch skillet over medium-low heat until a deep golden brown, about 20 minutes. If the onion does not turn color, add the teaspoon of sugar.

Add the garlic and sherry to the onion and cook until the garlic just turns tender (just when it starts to release its fragrance). Do not let the garlic burn. Season with salt and pepper.

Whisk the eggs, milk, salt, and pepper with a fork until just combined.

If necessary, add 1 to 2 tablespoons of olive oil or butter to the onion mixture.

Add the eggs to the pan and lower the heat to medium-low. Swirl the eggs so they cover the entire bottom of the pan.

After the edges of the egg begin to set, about 5 minutes, loosen them gently with a spatula, and then put the pan into the oven for 10 to 12 minutes. (How long you should cook the frittata will depend on how many eggs you use and the size of your pan.) The frittata is complete when the eggs have puffed and the top is slightly springy to the touch, like a cheesecake. The result is very much like a soufflé.

Let the frittata rest for about 10 minutes before slicing and serving it. Garnish with chopped parsley.

A TIP FROM MY MOTHER. Fried parsley is a great garnish for this dish.

Finger Paint Frittata

I have vivid memories of my very first omelet. I was just days old, swaddled securely in a cream-colored wicker bassinette on a faded yellow Formica countertop. My mother was at the stove, swearing and cursing and using words I had never heard. (Well, actually, that was true of most words.) Who knew the search for the perfect omelet would also improve my vocabulary?

I don't really remember my first omelet. I made that up. But my first *frittata*—that is a different story. My mother used to make something like this frittata when I was very young. The canvas is yellow (of course), and purees of bell peppers and spinach give red and green with which to paint. Dalí and Warhol made omelets art, and now so can you. Unlike most frittatas, this is not one to finish under the broiler or to invert or flip—the high heat tends to wash out the bright colors.

....

Serves 4

Master Technique: Flat/Frittata

2 tablespoons olive oil or unsalted butter
8 eggs, mixed
½ cup whole milk
Salt and freshly ground black pepper
¼ cup Puree of Spinach (recipe follows) or pesto
¼ cup Puree of Red Bell Pepper (recipe follows)
1 tablespoon chopped fresh flat-leaf parsley for garnish

Preheat the oven to 350°F. Heat the olive oil in an ovenproof 10- or 12-inch skillet until it shimmers, over medium heat.

Whisk the eggs, milk, salt, and black pepper with a fork until just combined.

Add the eggs to the pan and lower the heat to medium-low. Swirl the eggs so they cover the entire bottom of the pan. Cook over low heat until the eggs set, about 5 minutes. If there is uncooked egg, lift an edge up and tilt the pan so the uncooked egg runs underneath the cooked egg.

Add the spinach and red pepper purees to the top of the omelet and spread them in any pattern you like with a spatula.

After the edges of the egg begin to set, loosen them gently with a spatula, and then put the pan into the oven for approximately 10 to 12 minutes. The frittata is done when the eggs have puffed and the top is slightly springy to the touch. Let the frittata rest for about 10 minutes before slicing and serving it. Garnish with chopped parsley.

Puree of Spinach

3 to 4 cups baby spinach or spinach leaves (about ½ pound)
1 teaspoon olive oil
1 garlic clove, minced
Salt and freshly ground black pepper

Sauté the spinach in a skillet in the olive oil over medium-low heat until wilted, about 2 minutes. Add the garlic and season with salt and pepper.

Puree the spinach in a blender or food processor until smooth. Adjust the seasonings. If the puree is too thick, thin it with a little stock or water.

Puree of Red Bell Pepper

1 red bell pepper (or orange bell pepper)
Salt and freshly ground black pepper

Preheat the oven to 425°F.

Slice the red pepper in half lengthwise from stem to stern and remove the seeds. Cut the pepper into thin strips. Toss with the tablespoon of olive oil and salt and black pepper. Place the pepper on a baking sheet and roast in the oven until tender, about 20 minutes.

Transfer the pepper to a blender or food processor with 1 teaspoon of olive oil from the roasting pan. Puree until smooth. Adjust the seasonings. If the puree is too thick, thin it with a little stock or water.

Variation: If time is a consideration, puree jarred red peppers with a little olive oil in a blender or food processor.

Frittata with Peas, Sun-Dried Tomatoes, and Mozzarella

For a sad while, back in the 1980s, one simply could not avoid sun-dried tomatoes. Some culinary deity, it seemed, had issued a kitchen commandment: Every new dish, and every timeworn recipe too, must incorporate sun-dried tomatoes or risk someone, somebody, or something's wrath. You can omit them from this dish without fear of angering me (or my mother), but they really do show well in this pretty frittata.

I like this frittata a lot, but I am not a big fan of peas. I once spent a miserable summer in Milton-Freewater, Oregon, working nights at a pea-processing plant. At the time Milton-Freewater was the self-described "pea capital of the world." By self-described, I mean the town proudly proclaimed its pea preeminence on a giant garish billboard on the town line. Milton-Freewater is a very nice place, but I've never gone back to visit.

....

SERVES 4
Master Technique: Frittata/Flat

8 eggs, mixed
½ cup whole milk
3 to 4 tablespoons chopped sun-dried tomatoes
1 ½ cups fresh or frozen peas
Salt and freshly ground black pepper
2 tablespoons olive oil or unsalted butter
½ pound fresh mozzarella, sliced thinly
Parsley sprig for garnish

Preheat the oven to 350°F.

Preheat a nonstick, ovenproof 10- or 12-inch skillet (a seasoned cast-iron skillet is also a good choice) over medium to medium-low heat.

Whisk the eggs, milk, tomatoes, peas, salt, and pepper with a fork until just combined.

Heat the olive oil, swirl to coat the pan, and when it shimmers, add the eggs. Swirl the eggs so they cover the entire bottom of the pan. Cook over low heat until the eggs set, about 5 minutes. If there is uncooked egg, lift an edge up and tilt the pan so the uncooked egg runs underneath the cooked egg.

After the edges of the egg begin to set, loosen them gently with a spatula, and then put the pan into the oven for approximately 10 to 12 minutes. (How long you should cook the frittata will depend on how many eggs you use and the size of your pan.)

About 5 minutes before the frittata is finished, layer the top of the eggs with the sliced mozzarella. Return to the oven until the cheese melts.

Let the frittata rest for about 10 minutes before slicing and serving it.

Garnish with a sprig of basil or parsley.

Variations: Whenever I see peas in a recipe, I think of ham or, in this case, prosciutto or pancetta, all of which would be a nice twist to this recipe. If you can't find sun-dried tomatoes, slow-roasted tomatoes are a good substitute.

Fiddlehead Frittata

Every spring, for a very brief while, you will see cars, trucks, and trailers pulled along the side of the road in rural Maine, busy about the business of buying and selling fiddleheads. Particularly tasty are the fiddleheads from Aroostook County in northern Maine. Are you unfamiliar with fiddleheads? A fiddlehead (there are several varieties) is a sort of fern, or better, the tip of the fronds of very young ferns, snipped before they unfurl into maturity. They are "fiddleheads" because the young fronds resemble a violin or a fiddle. One must eat them when they are just picked and very fresh. They taste vaguely of asparagus, which is a passable substitute in this recipe.

SERVES 4
Master Technique: Frittata/Flat

4 to 5 small fiddleheads
Salt and freshly ground black pepper
1 teaspoon fresh lemon juice
1 teaspoon olive oil
1 teaspoon minced garlic (optional)
8 eggs, mixed
2 tablespoons white wine
2 tablespoons unsalted butter or olive oil
Fresh herbs for garnish

If there is any brown residue on your fiddleheads, remove it under a gentle spray from the faucet.

Cook the fiddleheads in lightly salted water in a large saucepot over a gentle boil until very tender, 7 to 8 minutes. Remove and drain. Season with salt, pepper, and the lemon juice.

Preheat the oven to 350°F.

Preheat a nonstick, ovenproof 10- or 12-inch skillet (a seasoned cast-iron skillet is also a good choice) over medium to medium-low heat.

Very lightly sauté the fiddleheads in 1 teaspoon of olive oil. If you like, a little minced garlic complements the taste of the ferns. Leave the fiddleheads in the pan.

Whisk the eggs, wine, salt, and pepper with a fork until just combined. Heat 2 tablespoons of butter, swirl to coat the pan, and when it shimmers, add the eggs. Cook over low heat until the eggs set, about 5 minutes.

After the edges of the egg begin to set, loosen them gently with a spatula, and then put the pan into the oven for approximately 10 to 12 minutes. (How long you should cook the frittata will depend on how many eggs you use and the size of your pan.) The frittata is complete when the eggs have puffed and the top is slightly springy to the touch.

Let the frittata rest for about 10 minutes before slicing and serving it. Garnish with fresh herbs.

Variations: Nothing tastes quite like a fresh fiddlehead, but young asparagus tips or dandelion greens would suit this frittata. One can also sometimes find jarred or canned fiddleheads. The taste is not quite the same, but they are fun to try.

A béarnaise or a béchamel sauce would make a nice accompaniment to this frittata.

Frittata with Spinach, Wild Mushrooms, and Goat Cheese

This is a delightful frittata for a formal luncheon or a brunch.

....

SERVES 4
Master Technique: Flat/Frittata

2 cups chopped wild mushrooms
2 to 3 tablespoons olive oil
1 tablespoon unsalted butter
2 garlic cloves, chopped
2 cups fresh baby spinach leaves
1 teaspoon freshly grated nutmeg
Salt and freshly ground black pepper
8 eggs, mixed
½ cup whole milk
1 tablespoon chopped fresh flat-leaf parsley
½ cup soft goat cheese
Fresh herbs for garnish

Preheat the oven to 350°F.

Cook the mushrooms in an ovenproof 10- to 12-inch skillet in 1 tablespoon of the olive oil and the butter over medium-high heat until they are deep brown.

Lower the heat to low and sauté the garlic with the mushrooms for 2 to 3 minutes.

Add the spinach leaves and cook until they wilt, just a minute or two. Season with the nutmeg, salt, and pepper. Leave in the pan.

Whisk the eggs, milk, parsley, salt, and pepper with a fork until just combined.

Add the eggs to the pan and set the heat to medium-low. Swirl the eggs so they cover the entire bottom of the pan. Cook over low heat until the eggs set, about 5 minutes.

If there is uncooked egg, lift an edge up and tilt the pan so the uncooked egg runs underneath the cooked egg.

After the edges of the egg begin to set, loosen them gently with a spatula, and then put the pan into the oven for approximately 10 to 12 minutes. (How long you should cook the frittata will depend on how many eggs you use and the size of your pan.) The frittata is complete when the eggs have puffed and the top is slightly springy to the touch.

About 5 minutes before the frittata is finished, top it with the crumbled goat cheese and return it to the oven to melt the cheese.

The frittata is complete when the cheese melts and the top is slightly springy to the touch.

Let the frittata rest for about 10 minutes before slicing and serving it. Garnish with fresh herbs.

Variation: Arugula is a nice understudy for spinach.

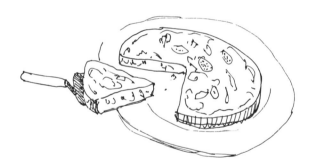

Frittata Salsa Verde with Fire-Roasted Jalapeño Peppers and Corn

Fresh salsa verde makes a big difference in this recipe, but a jarred salsa also serves quite well. Do roast the jalapeños and corn. It takes a little effort, but taking the time and trouble is an essential part of the philosophy of the perfect omelet.

....

SERVES 4
Master Technique: Flat/Frittata

8 eggs, mixed
1 cup salsa verde (recipe follows)
2 small green jalapeño peppers, roasted, skinned, and minced
2 cups corn kernels, roasted
2 or 3 drops green Tabasco
Salt and freshly ground black pepper
2 tablespoons olive oil
1 tablespoon sour cream for garnish
Cilantro sprig for garnish

Preheat the oven to 350°F.

Preheat an ovenproof 10- to 12-inch pan over medium heat.

Whisk the eggs, ½ cup of the salsa verde, jalapeño, corn, Tabasco, salt, and black pepper with a fork until just combined.

Heat the olive oil, swirl to coat the pan, and when it shimmers, add the eggs. Lower the heat to medium-low. Swirl the eggs so they cover the entire bottom of the pan. Cook over low heat until the eggs set, about 5 minutes. If there is uncooked egg, lift an edge up and tilt the pan so the uncooked egg runs underneath the cooked egg.

After the edges of the egg begin to set, loosen them gently with a spatula, and then put the pan into the oven for 10 to 12 minutes. (How long you should cook the frittata will depend on how many eggs you use and the size of your pan.) The frittata is complete when the eggs have puffed and the top is slightly springy to the touch.

Let the frittata rest for about 10 minutes before slicing and serving it. Garnish with the remaining ½ cup of salsa verde spread out over the top of the eggs, a dollop of sour cream, and a sprig of cilantro.

Roasted Salsa Verde

A simple salsa verde should be a staple in your kitchen. It makes a wonderful accompaniment to a great variety of dishes, including eggs. This version takes a recipe by well-known chef Rick Bayless as its inspiration.

6 ounces (about 4 medium) tomatillos, husked and rinsed
2 green chiles (jalapeno or serrano), seeded and finely diced, to taste
1 clove garlic
4 sprigs fresh cilantro, roughly chopped
¼ cup finely chopped white onion
Zest of ½ lime
Juice of ½ lime
White wine (optional)
Salt and freshly ground black pepper

Preheat the broiler.

Roast the tomatillos and chiles on a baking sheet in a very hot broiler until the skin on the tomatillos begins to blister and blacken. Turn the tomatillos and peppers and blacken the other side.

Process the tomatillos, chiles, garlic, cilantro, onions, and lime juice and zest in a food processor. If necessary, thin the puree with a little white wine or water. Season with salt and pepper to taste.

Marina's Frittina
with Caramelized Shallots,
Chives, and Balsamic Vinegar

One summer in Veneto, I struck up a conversation with an accomplished cook who was leading a hands-on demonstration of pasta making for a small group of enthusiastic American visitors. While teaching us how to roll out fresh gnocchi, Marina whipped up these frittinas to snack on. A frittina, I learned, is sort of a mini frittata, usually made in a mini muffin pan.

....

MAKES 24 FRITTINAS
Master Technique: Flat/Frittata

Olive or canola oil spray for pan
3 large (about 6 ounces total) shallots, peeled, halved, and sliced
1 tablespoon unsalted butter
1 teaspoon sugar (optional)
Salt and freshly ground black pepper
8 eggs, mixed
⅓ cup whole milk or ricotta cheese
2 tablespoons finely chopped fresh chives
1 teaspoon balsamic vinegar
Parmesan Tuiles for garnish (optional, page 000)
Parmagiano-Reggiano curls for garnish (optional)

Preheat the oven to 400°F.

Spray a 24-well mini-muffin pan with olive or canola oil.

Sauté the shallots in a skillet with the butter over medium heat until they turn brown, 6 to 8 minutes. If they do not turn, add a little sugar and cook a bit longer. Season with salt and pepper and set aside.

Whisk the eggs, milk, chives, balsamic vinegar, shallots, salt, and pepper with a fork until just combined.

Pour the eggs into the prepared muffin pan, filling each well about two-thirds full.

Bake approximately for 8 to 10 minutes. The frittinas are finished when they puff and the tops are golden brown. Remove and cool on a wire rack.

Serve immediately on a platter and drizzle with balsamic vinegar. Garnish with Parmesan Tuiles or with shaved Parmigiano-Reggiano curls.

Variations: Spinach is a lovely, colorful addition to these mini-frittatas, as are very finely chopped red and green bell peppers. These are also superb with fresh grated cheese and fresh herbs.

Potato Tortilla

Tortilla de patatas

This potato omelet might be the national dish of Spain. It certainly has a long history. There are recipes for a Tortilla de patatas in the notebooks of Francisco Martinez Montino, head chef for two Hapsburg kings and author of one of the most important cookbooks in Spanish history, *Arte de cocina,* published in 1611. Sliced into small wedges and served at room temperature, the tortilla is a staple in tapas bars. At lunch they are a *pincho,* "a slightly larger slice served with a piece of bread."

....

SERVES 4
Master Technique: Flat/Tortilla

1 ½ pounds potatoes, peeled and sliced very thinly (preferably a soft potato,
    such as russet)
¼ cup olive oil
8 eggs
Salt and freshly ground black pepper
2 tablespoons water or white wine
Fresh fruit for garnish

Preheat a 10- or 12-inch skillet over medium heat.

Sauté the potatoes in ¼ cup of the olive oil until they are soft and tender, but do not brown them, about 15 to 18 minutes. Season with salt and pepper and set aside. Reserve 2 tablespoons of oil in the pan.

Whisk the eggs, water, salt, and pepper with a fork until just combined. Gently add the sliced potatoes to the eggs and let them soak for about 10 minutes.

If necessary, add 1 to 2 tablespoons of the reserved olive oil to the pan, swirl to coat the pan, and when it shimmers, add the eggs. Lower the heat to low and cook until the eggs set, approximately 10 to 12 minutes, shaking the pan occasionally to make sure the eggs are not sticking. If there is uncooked egg, lift an edge up and tilt the pan so the uncooked egg runs underneath the cooked egg.

When the top of the eggs begin to set and are nearly firm, invert the tortilla onto a plate. Make sure the plate is bigger than the tortilla! If you invert the tortilla before the top of the eggs begin to set, you'll end up with quite the mess. If the eggs seem reluctant to set, cover the pan for a minute or two to help them along.

Return the tortilla to the pan over medium heat to finish cooking, adding an additional teaspoon of olive oil if necessary. Cook for about an additional 2 to 3 minutes, until the tortilla is firm. A tortilla, unlike a frittata, may be flipped or turned two or three times. The inverted top should be golden brown.

Let the tortilla rest for about 10 minutes before slicing and serving it. Garnish with fresh fruit.

Variations: Like frittatas, tortillas come in endless kinds, and can vary tremendously from region to region in Spain and Portugal. A tortilla with rice and ham is favored in Valencia, and another with local asparagus is popular in Madrid. Some of my favorites are made with sardines (Tortilla de sardinas), with spinach and garlic (Tortilla de espinacas), and with wild mushrooms (Tortilla a la cazadora).

Tortilla española

Some folks think the Tortilla de patatas eventually became the Tortilla española. To keep them distinct, I include onions in the latter recipe—a matter of some discussion among Spaniards, from what I can gather. A Tortilla española is especially good as an appetizer or a light dinner.

....

SERVES 4
Master Technique: Flat/Tortilla

½ cup thinly sliced yellow onion
1 tablespoon olive oil, plus more as needed
1 tablespoon unsalted butter
Salt and freshly ground black pepper
1 ½ pounds potatoes, peeled and sliced very thinly
8 eggs, mixed
2 tablespoons water or white wine
Mint for garnish
Fresh fruit for garnish

Preheat a 10- or 12-inch skillet over medium heat.

Sauté the onion in 1 tablespoon of olive oil and the butter over medium-low heat until tender and translucent. Season with salt and pepper and set aside.

In the same pan, sauté the potatoes (add additional olive oil, if necessary) over medium-low heat until they are tender, but do not brown them, 15 to 18 minutes. Season with salt and pepper and set aside.

Whisk the eggs, water, salt, and pepper with a fork until just combined. Gently add the sliced potatoes and onion to the eggs and let them soak for about 10 minutes.

If necessary, add 1 to 2 tablespoons of olive oil to the pan, swirl to coat the pan, and when it shimmers, add the eggs. Lower the heat to low and cook until the eggs set, 10 to 12 minutes, shaking the pan occasionally to make sure the eggs are not sticking.

If there is uncooked egg, lift an edge up and tilt the pan so the uncooked egg runs underneath the cooked egg.

When the top of the eggs begin to set and are nearly firm, invert the tortilla onto a plate. Make sure the plate is bigger than the tortilla!

Return the tortilla to the pan over medium heat to finish cooking, adding an additional teaspoon of olive oil, if necessary. Cook for about an additional 2 to 3 minutes, until the tortilla is firm. A tortilla, unlike a frittata, may be flipped or turned two or three times. The inverted top should be golden brown.

Let the tortilla rest for about 10 minutes before slicing and serving it. Garnish with mint and fresh fruit.

Tortilla with Ham and Mint

Tortilla a la Navarra

I first encountered this recipe at a small tapas bar in Madrid, and Penelope Casas has a recipe for a similar tortilla in her wonderful cookbook on regional Spanish cooking, entitled *Delicioso!* My version uses both as inspiration. Navarre is a region in northern Spain with a rich culinary cultural heritage. It is well known for its wines, especially its rosés.

SERVES 4
Master Technique: Flat/Tortilla

1 pound red potatoes, sliced thinly
¼ cup olive oil
¼ cup finely chopped onion
Salt and freshly ground black pepper
6 eggs, mixed
1 tablespoon rosé wine
4 ounces cured ham, diced
2 cloves garlic, minced
1 tablespoon chopped fresh flat-leaf parsley
1 tablespoon chopped fresh mint
Mint sprig for garnish

Sauté the potatoes in a skillet in ¼ cup of olive oil over medium-low heat for about 15 minutes, until tender but not brown.

Add the onion and cook until translucent. Season with salt and pepper, drain, and set aside. Reserve 2 tablespoons of oil in the pan.

Whisk the eggs, wine, ham, garlic, parsley, mint, salt, and pepper with a fork until just combined.

Gently add the sliced potatoes and onions to the eggs and let them soak for about 10 minutes.

If necessary, add 1 to 2 tablespoons of the reserved olive oil to the pan, swirl to coat the pan, and when it shimmers, add the eggs. Lower the heat to low and cook until the eggs set, 10 to 12 minutes, shaking the pan occasionally to make sure the eggs are not sticking. If there is uncooked egg, lift an edge up and tilt the pan so the uncooked egg runs underneath the cooked egg.

When the top of the eggs begin to set and are nearly firm, invert the tortilla onto a plate. Make sure the plate is bigger than the tortilla!

Return the tortilla to the pan over medium heat to finish cooking, adding an additional teaspoon of olive oil, if necessary. Cook for about an additional 2 to 3 minutes, until the tortilla is firm. A tortilla, unlike a frittata, may be flipped or turned two or three times. The inverted top should be golden brown.

Let the tortilla rest for about 10 minutes before slicing and serving it. Garnish with a sprig of mint.

Tortilla with Garlic and Parsley

One of the unwritten rules of tortilla cookery seems to be that a true tortilla must include potatoes and may include onions. This tortilla includes neither, so maybe it is not really a tortilla, in the classic sense, but I first chanced upon it in a hotel bar in Madrid. (There, perhaps, is the proof that this tortilla is inauthentic, marketed as it was to tourists.) Whatever its claim to authenticity, it is delicious and, in its simplicity of ingredients, an honorable and dutiful tribute to the tortilla.

SERVES 4
Master Technique: Tortilla/Flat

8 eggs
4 tablespoons chopped fresh flat-leaf parsley
4 garlic cloves, chopped
1 tablespoon white wine
Salt and freshly ground black pepper
2 tablespoons olive oil
Parsley sprig for garnish

Preheat a 10- to 12-inch skillet over medium heat.

Whisk the eggs, parsley, garlic, wine, salt, and pepper with a fork until just combined.

Place 1 to 2 tablespoons of the olive oil in the pan, swirl to coat the pan, and when it shimmers, add the eggs. Lower the heat to low and cook until the eggs set, approximately 10 to 12 minutes, shaking the pan occasionally to make sure the eggs are not sticking. If there is uncooked egg, lift an edge up and tilt the pan so the uncooked egg runs underneath the cooked egg.

When the top of the eggs begin to set and are nearly firm, invert the tortilla onto a plate. Make sure the plate is bigger than the tortilla!

Return the tortilla to the pan over medium heat to finish cooking, adding an additional teaspoon of olive oil if necessary. Cook for about an additional 2 to 3 minutes, until the tortilla is firm. A tortilla, unlike a frittata, may be flipped or turned two or three times. The inverted top should be golden brown.

Let the tortilla rest for about 10 minutes before slicing and serving it. Garnish with a sprig of parsley.

....

Variations: The combination of fresh parsley and garlic is a *persillade* in French cuisine. It is similar to a chimichurri sauce, common in Argentina and other South American countries, and a staple in many other national and regional cuisines. It can be varied simply by adding or substituting different spices or by adding a teaspoon of a flavored vinegar. Add lemon zest and it becomes a gremolata. Add bread crumbs and it is a fine crust for meat, chicken, or fish.

....

A TIP FROM MY MOTHER: Fried parsley and half a head of roasted garlic is just the right garnish for this dish.

Stuffed Thai Omelet

Khai Yat Sai

A *khai yat sai*, sometimes spelled *kha yad sai*, is a stuffed omelet from Thailand, usually filled with a spiced minced meat and colorful, highly seasoned vegetables. In traditional form, the eggs are very thin, like a crepe, and stuffed thick. A word in advance: This is a big omelet!

....

SERVES 3 TO 4
Master Technique: American/Folded

1 tablespoon olive or vegetable oil
⅓ pound ground pork
⅓ pound ground turkey, beef, or veal
½ cup chopped onion
1 garlic clove
1 teaspoon minced fresh ginger
1 small hot pepper (jalapeño or serrano or similar), chopped finely
⅓ cup diced tomato
1 green onion, sliced thinly
1 teaspoon minced fresh lemongrass
1 teaspoon finely chopped fresh chives
Salt and freshly ground black pepper
1 tablespoon oyster sauce, or to taste
Cornstarch or arrowroot (optional)
5 eggs, mixed
1 tablespoon water or oyster sauce
2 tablespoons unsalted butter or olive oil
Chopped scallions for garnish

Heat the tablespoon of oil in a 10- or 12-inch skillet until it shimmers, over medium to medium-high heat.

Add the pork and turkey, crumbling it with a spatula or spoon as it cooks.

Before the meat turns brown, add the onion to the same pan and cook until translucent.

Add the garlic, ginger, hot pepper, tomato, green onion, lemongrass, and chives and cook until tender, about 5 minutes. Add salt, black pepper, and oyster sauce, and season to taste. If the mixture is runny, thicken it with a little cornstarch or arrowroot. Set aside and keep warm.

Preheat a 10- to 12-inch skillet over medium heat.

Whisk the eggs, water or oyster sauce, salt, and black pepper with a fork until just combined.

Add the butter to the pan, swirl to coat the pan, and when it shimmers, add the eggs. Swirl the eggs so they cover the entire bottom of the pan. Let the eggs sit quietly for about 10 seconds.

Holding the handle of the pan and using a spatula, pull the uncooked egg toward the center of the pan, proceeding calmly and deliberately around the compass, north to south to east to west. Use a spatula to lift the eggs from the rim of the pan, and move the remaining uncooked egg under the cooked portion.

Let the omelet cook for a minute or two, occasionally moving the uncooked egg under the cooked portion as necessary. The omelet should be very thin, almost like a crepe.

When the eggs have set, add the meat mixture to the center of the omelet. Using a spatula, fold the omelet in half, moving from the outside of the pan to the inside.

Turn out the omelet onto a warm plate. Garnish with chopped scallions.

Japanese Omelet with Scallions

Tamagoyaki with Scallions

A *tamagoyaki* is a Japanese omelet prepared in a rectangular pan called a *maki-yakinabe*. The omelet is composed of several thin layers of egg. It is then placed on a small bamboo mat (often sold with the pan), which is used to roll the omelet tightly into a cylindrical shape. If you do not have a square or rectangular pan, you can still adopt the basic method—it will not look quite the same, but you will get a sense of the dish. (In this recipe, I assume you will be using your round omelet pan.) Most recipes for tamagoyaki flavor the eggs with soy sauce, sugar, and sometimes sake or mirin. For something much less close to the original, but still quite tasty, make a traditional French (rolled) omelet, but replace the water with shoyu. Tamagoyaki is often much sweeter than this recipe calls for, so adjust to your taste. Because it may be eaten warm or at room temperature, a tamagoyaki makes an excellent lunch, as anyone who has ever ordered a take-away bento box knows.

....

SERVES 1
Master Technique: French/Rolled

4 eggs, mixed
2 tablespoons finely chopped scallion
1 teaspoon shoyu
1 teaspoon sugar
1 teaspoon freshly ground white pepper
2 tablespoons unsalted butter

Whisk the eggs, scallions, shoyu, sugar, and white pepper in a large measuring bowl or a mixing bowl with a spout.

Heat the butter in an 8- to 9-inch pan over medium-low heat. When the butter sizzles, add about one-quarter of the egg mixture to the butter—it should be very thin. Let the eggs sit still until they begin to set on the bottom, but are not yet fully cooked on top. The egg cooks very quickly.

With a spatula (or chopsticks), gently roll the eggs to one edge of the pan and leave them there.

If necessary, add a little more butter to the pan, and another one-quarter of the eggs. Make sure the eggs cover the entire bottom of the pan, including under the eggs you have already cooked and rolled. After the new eggs have begun to set on the bottom, but are not yet fully cooked on top, roll the first eggs back across the pan, picking up the new layer.

Repeat until you have used all the egg mixture. If you have a bamboo mat, place the omelet on it and roll it up tightly. I have tried to use parchment paper, sprayed with olive oil, to mimic the effect, but it doesn't seem to work for me. If you prefer, simply plate the omelet straight from the pan, slice it into thin pieces on the bias, and garnish.

Variations: One very common variation is to layer a small piece of nori over each layer of egg as it cooks. The result is a striking layered contrast of colors. Another very common variation, called a Dashimaki Tamagoyaki, is to use dashi, a sort of stock often made from kelp and a few other ingredients, instead of shoyu. It is not very traditional, but I like to add very finely minced red and green bell peppers to the egg mixture.

Japanese Omelet with Chicken, Rice, and Ketchup

Omurice

An *omurice* is a home-style omelet made with fried rice, a few other ingredients, and served with ketchup. It is very popular in Japan, parts of South Korea, and Taiwan. It is also a staple on kids' menus, or *okosama-ranchi*. However, it is not just a children's food. Upscale versions sometimes replace the ketchup with a béchamel or a demi-glace, but first try it with ketchup.

....

SERVES 1
Master Technique: American/Folded

1 teaspoon olive oil
¼ cup finely chopped onion
⅓ pound ground chicken
¼ cup cooked brown rice (or leftover fried rice from last night's takeout)
1 teaspoon ketchup, plus more for garnish
Salt and freshly ground black pepper
2 eggs, mixed
1 tablespoon water
1 tablespoon unsalted butter

Preheat a nonstick, 9- to 10-inch skillet over medium to medium-high heat.

Add the olive oil to the pan, and when it shimmers, add the onion. Sauté the onion until it is translucent and soft.

Add the chicken to the onion and cook until the chicken is no longer pink and begins to brown.

Add the cooked rice and ketchup to the pan and cook until heated through. Season with salt and pepper and set aside.

Preheat an 8- or 9-inch skillet over medium heat.

Whisk the eggs, water, salt, and pepper with a fork until just combined.

Melt the butter in the skillet, swirl to coat the pan, and when the butter sizzles, add the eggs. Swirl the eggs so they cover the entire bottom of the pan. Let the eggs sit quietly for about 10 seconds.

Holding the handle of the pan and using a spatula, pull the uncooked egg toward the center of the pan, proceeding calmly and deliberately around the compass, north to south to east to west. Use a spatula to lift the eggs from the rim of the pan, and move the remaining uncooked egg under the cooked portion.

Let the omelet cook for a minute or two, occasionally moving the uncooked egg under the cooked portion as necessary.

When the eggs have set, add chicken mixture to the center of the omelet. Using a spatula, fold the omelet in half, moving from the outside of the pan to the inside.

Turn out the omelet onto a warm plate. Decorate the top of the omelet with additional ketchup.

Variation: Adding 2 tablespoons of ketchup directly into the egg mixture gives the eggs a delightfully unusual color.

Shrimp and Crab Egg Foo Yong

There is much dispute about how to spell egg foo yong (and about how to prepare it), but pretty much everyone agrees that its origins lay in a traditional Cantonese dish, altered substantially by Chinese immigrants to California in the 1850s. James Beard thought it was the inspiration for the western (Denver) omelet. It may be prepared with shrimp, pork, or chicken, and it always includes a rich assortment of thinly sliced vegetables. I use shrimp because that is how my father always ordered it at the only Chinese restaurant in town. Egg foo yong is typically served with a simple brown sauce.

....

SERVES 2
Master Technique: American/Folded

Sauce:
1 tablespoon unsalted butter
1 tablespoon all-purpose flour
¾ to 1 cup vegetable, chicken, or fish stock
1 teaspoon sherry or shoyu
Salt and freshly ground black pepper

Eggs:
2 tablespoons chopped celery
2 tablespoons chopped onion
1 tablespoon shredded or julienned carrot
1 tablespoon chopped bok choy
1 scallion, chopped
1 mushroom, sliced
1 tablespoon olive oil
½ cup cooked small shrimp (about 12 ounces), chopped, reserving a few whole
    shrimp for garnish
¼ cup (4 to 6 ounces) cooked crabmeat
1 tablespoon bean sprouts
Salt and freshly ground black pepper
4 eggs, mixed

1 tablespoon shoyu
1 tablespoon butter
Chives or chopped scallions for garnish

Prepare the sauce: Make a roux with the butter and flour in a small saucepan. When the flour is sandy, add ¼ cup of the stock and whisk vigorously. Slowly add the remaining stock until fully incorporated. Season with sherry, salt, and pepper. Keep warm.

Prepare the eggs: Over medium heat, sauté the celery, onion, carrots, bok choy, scallion, and mushrooms in the olive oil in a 10-inch skillet until tender and translucent.

Add the shrimp, crabmeat, and bean sprouts and cook until warm and the shrimp are no longer pink. Season with salt and pepper and set aside.

Preheat a nonstick, 8 or 9-inch skillet over medium to medium-high heat.

Whisk the eggs, shoyu, salt, and pepper with a fork until just combined.

Melt the butter in the skillet, swirl to coat the pan, and when the butter sizzles, add the eggs. Swirl the eggs so they cover the entire bottom of the pan. Let the eggs sit quietly for about 10 seconds.

Holding the handle of the pan and using a spatula, pull the uncooked egg toward the center of the pan, proceeding calmly and deliberately around the compass, north to south to east to west. Use a spatula to lift the eggs from the rim of the pan, and move the remaining uncooked egg under the cooked portion.

When the eggs have set, add the shrimp mixture to the center of the omelet.

Using a spatula, fold the omelet in half, moving from the outside of the pan to the inside. Turn out the omelet onto a warm plate.

Spoon the sauce over and around the omelet, top with a few of the reserved whole shrimp, and garnish with chopped chives or scallions.

Variation: Many recipes for egg foo yong fold the meat (pork, ham, or chicken) and vegetables into the eggs before frying the eggs in the pan like a pancake or crab cake.

Middle Eastern
Omelet with Fresh Herbs

Kuku Sabzi

A very traditional, and verdant, Persian flat omelet abundant with herbs is the inspiration for this recipe. I have suggested parsley, chives, cilantro, and, somewhat unusually, mint, but you might try any green herb, including dill, sage, marjoram, basil, or chervil. It is nearly impossible to use too many herbs in this omelet. The finished version should be more green than yellow.

Like frittatas and tortillas, kukus can be served hot or cold.

SERVES 4
Master Recipe: Flat/Frittata

8 eggs, mixed
2 tablespoons chopped fresh flat-leaf parsley
2 tablespoons finely chopped fresh chives
1 tablespoon chopped fresh cilantro
2 tablespoons chopped fresh mint
2 scallions, chopped
2 tablespoons water or Greek yogurt
Salt and freshly ground black pepper
2 tablespoons unsalted butter or olive oil
Chives or scallions for garnish
Mint sprig for garnish

Preheat the oven to 350°F.

Preheat a nonstick, ovenproof 10- or 12-inch skillet (a seasoned cast-iron skillet is also a good choice) over medium to medium-low heat.

Whisk the eggs, parsley, chives, cilantro, mint, scallions, water or yogurt, salt, and pepper with a fork until just combined.

Heat the butter, swirl to coat the pan, and when it shimmers, add the eggs. Cook over low heat until the eggs set, about 5 minutes. If there is uncooked egg, lift an edge up and tilt the pan so the uncooked egg runs underneath the cooked egg.

After the edges of the egg begin to set, loosen them gently with a spatula, and then put the pan into the oven for approximately 10 to 12 minutes. (How long you should cook the frittata will depend on how many eggs you use and the size of your pan.) The kuku is done when the eggs have puffed and the top is slightly springy to the touch.

Garnish with chopped chives or scallions and a sprig of mint placed in the center of the kuku.

Variations: Chopped walnuts are a great addition to this omelet, as are dried fruits, such as apricots. Kukus also often incorporate eggplant or potato. In Afghan cuisine, a kuku is called a *khagina* and may be made with eggplant, tomatoes, or leeks (*gandana*).

Persian Eggplant Omelet
Kuku-ye Bademjan

This is one of my favorite omelets. I learned it from a fellow student in culinary school. She would whip up several of these for "family meal," a ritualistic occasion where students just new to the restaurant kitchen cooked for the entire staff. All too often, this became a good-natured competition to see which class could outdo the others. You can also cook this omelet in the oven, like a frittata. Some folks suggest that you dice and salt the eggplant and place in a colander if you think it may be bitter.

. . . .

SERVES 4
Master Technique: Flat/Frittata

2 cups diced eggplant
½ cup chopped onion
1 cup sliced zucchini
Salt and freshly ground black pepper
2 tablespoons olive oil
1 teaspoon ground turmeric
1 teaspoon ground cinnamon
6 eggs, mixed
1 tablespoon chopped fresh flat-leaf parsley
2 tablespoons water
1 tablespoon unsalted butter or olive oil
Mint or basil sprig for garnish

Preheat the broiler.

Preheat a nonstick, ovenproof 10- or 12-inch skillet (a seasoned cast-iron skillet is also a good choice) over medium to medium-low heat.

Lightly sauté the eggplant, onion, and zucchini with salt and pepper in 2 tablespoons of olive oil until the vegetables are tender. Add the turmeric and cinnamon and stir gently to incorporate the spices. Season with salt and pepper.

Whisk the eggs, parsley, water, salt, and pepper with a fork until just combined.

Add a tablespoon of butter, if necessary, swirl to coat the pan, and when it shimmers, add the eggs to the eggplant mixture. Cook over low heat until the eggs set, approximately 6 to 8 minutes. If there is uncooked egg, lift an edge up and tilt the pan so the uncooked egg runs underneath the cooked egg.

Finish the kuku under the broiler until the eggs are firm and are slightly brown, perhaps a minute or two.

Garnish with a sprig of mint or basil.

Eggah with Garlic, Potato, and Parsley

Eggahs resemble tortillas and like tortillas may be served hot, warm, or cold, as an appetizer or a meal. Many have a form and appearance that is close to a fried pancake, in which, as Claudia Roden notes, the egg is more of a binder than the chief ingredient. This recipe uses more eggs and results in a very hearty flat omelet.

....

SERVES 4
Master Technique: Flat/Tortilla

2 tablespoons olive oil
2 cups thinly sliced parboiled potato
2 garlic cloves, chopped
Salt and freshly ground black pepper
8 eggs, mixed
2 tablespoons water
½ cup chopped fresh flat-leaf parsley, plus more for garnish
1 to 2 tablespoons unsalted butter (optional)
Chopped parsley for garnish

Heat the olive oil in a 10- or 12-inch skillet until it shimmers, over medium heat. Fry the potato until a deep golden brown. (You may need to do this in two batches.)

Add the garlic and sauté for 1 to 2 minutes. Season with salt and pepper.

Whisk the eggs, water, parsley, salt, and pepper with a fork until just combined.

If necessary, add 1 to 2 tablespoons of butter to the pan. Add the eggs and lower the heat to medium-low. Swirl the eggs so they cover the entire bottom of the pan. Cook over low heat until the eggs set, about 10 minutes. If there is uncooked egg, lift an edge up and tilt the pan so the uncooked egg runs underneath the cooked egg.

When the top of the eggs are nearly firm, slide the eggah onto a dinner plate, and then invert it back to the pan over medium-low heat to finish cooking, perhaps 3 to 4 minutes. The inverted top should be golden brown.

Garnish with chopped parsley.

***

Variations: Spinach instead of parsley works very well in this recipe. You might replace the potatoes with zucchini or eggplant.

In *The New Book of Middle Eastern Food*, Claudia Roden includes a similar omelet called Maacouda bi Batata. Her version uses onion rather than garlic and mashes the potatoes, combines them with just three eggs and the onion, and then briefly fries the potato and egg mixture before finishing it under the broiler.

***

Eggah with Mint, Tomato, and Bread

Mint and tomato may not be as common as basil and tomato, but it is just as delicious.

....

SERVES 4
Master Technique: Flat/Tortilla

1 cup very finely diced croutons
3 to 4 tablespoons olive oil
1 tablespoon unsalted butter
8 eggs, mixed
1 cup roughly chopped plum tomato (about 2 large), plus more for garnish
½ cup chopped fresh mint, plus more for garnish
2 tablespoons water
Salt and freshly ground black pepper
Mint sprig for garnish
Diced tomato for garnish

Toast the croutons in 1 tablespoon of the olive oil and the butter in a 10- or 12-inch skillet over medium heat.

Whisk the eggs, tomatoes, mint, water, salt, and pepper with a fork until just combined.

Add another tablespoon or two of oil to the pan (because the croutons soak up the oil) and lower the heat to medium-low.

Add the eggs to the pan. Swirl the eggs so they cover the entire bottom of the pan. Cook over low heat until the eggs set, about 10 minutes. If there is uncooked egg, lift an edge up and tilt the pan so the uncooked egg runs underneath the cooked egg.

When the top of the eggs are nearly firm, slide the eggah onto a dinner plate, and then invert it back to the pan over medium-low heat to finish cooking, perhaps 3 to 4 minutes. The inverted top should be golden brown.

Garnish with a sprig of mint and diced tomato.

Chapter Five:
Sweet & Spirited Omelets

———◦❙◉❙◦———

Dessert is completely inessential to life . . .
And yet is completely at the center of life.

—ADAM GOPNIK, *THE TABLE COMES FIRST*

They are not nearly as common now, but especially in the late 18th century and long into the nineteenth, well-to-do restaurants often featured a variety of "surprise omelets" as dishes on their dessert menus. Adolphe Meyer's comprehensive *Eggs in a Thousand Ways: A Guide for the Preparation of Eggs for the Table*, published in 1917, includes an entire section on such omelets, with nine recipes. Escoffier included eight recipes for surprise omelets, but noted, too, "With the general example given this kind of omelet may be indefinitely varied . . ."

In French cuisine, any dish *en surprise* means a dish prepared in a way to beguile the diner, often by hiding something—think of a hollowed fruit, filled with sorbet or ice cream and topped with its original "lid" or with a meringue or pastry—or by making a dish look like something it is not. So the "surprise" in an omelet surprise is that the dish is not an omelet at all, but rather a confectionary made to look like an omelet. Most omelets en surprise start with a genoise cake, often soaked with liqueur, covered with a layer of ice cream and a layer of fruit, all encased in a baked meringue.

An omelet en surprise was typically an elaborate affair, perfectly suited to the excesses of haute cuisine. Consider, for example, an Omelette surprise Mount Vesuvius. This concoction starts with a sponge cake, topped "with coneshaped alternate layers of strawberry and vanilla ice," which in turn was covered with an Italian meringue flavored with Kirshwasser. It sounds delicious if gilded, but still the omelet was not done: "With the aid of a pastry bag make a sort of container from the meringue preparation, and when the omelette is baked, fill it with stoned cherries stewed with currant jelly; pour over Kirshwasser and set fire to it before serving."

Another such omelet, an Omelette surprise Pompadour, was a favorite of Jacqueline Kennedy and served on more than one occasion in the

White House. It sounds oh so very French, but it was perfectly suited to America's First Lady and to the first kitchen. Indeed, the most famous of "surprise" desserts, Baked Alaska, is of distinctly American origin and not French at all. Many culinary historians associate Baked Alaska with the great chef at Delmonico's, Charles Ranhofer, who invented the dish in tribute to the purchase of Alaska from Russia in 1867 (he called it "Alaska, Florida"). Perhaps more surprising, the roots of Baked Alaska go back much further in American history, to a state dinner in Thomas Jefferson's White House that featured a dessert of ice cream encased in pastry. A nearly contemporaneous French version is the well-known Omelette à la norvegienne, dated to 1891.

Since these "omelets" are often just cake and ice cream, we are entitled to ask whether surprise omelets are really omelets. I refer you back to our discussion of omelet philosophy in the introduction, but here the operative principle appears to be that if it looks vaguely like an omelet, and if you can be tricked to think it is an omelet (when really it is not), then it is an omelet. No one ever falls for the trick, but it is rude not to play along.

For most of us, the true surprise is the very idea that an omelet (a real one, not an imposter) might be a dessert at all. It shouldn't really be so startling when we consider that eggs are a key ingredient in so many different dessert dishes, and the chief ingredient in more than a few—think of a tantalizing mousse, a lacy crepe, or a delicate, airy soufflé. Generally composed of beaten egg whites folded into a foundation of yolks 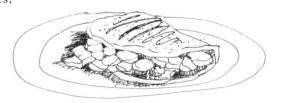 and various flavorings, a soufflé is baked in a fast oven. The heat causes the air bubbles in the whipped whites to expand, giving the soufflé its impressive height and delicate composition. Soufflés should certainly not be confined to desserts, but as desserts, they are quite versatile. They may be iced, chilled, or baked and made with chocolates, fruits, liqueurs, or nuts.

Like their royal relative, soufflé omelets (sometimes called puffy omelets) and mousseline omelets may be savory or sweet. They are often served with liqueurs or sweet jams or with candied fruits and nuts. Some are unassuming and homey, like an omelet with macerated fresh fruit, where others are intricate and showy, like an Omelette aux pommes flambées.

In this chapter, I present several recipes for sweet omelets, all in keeping with the philosophy of the perfect omelet, that challenge readers to rethink the idea of what an omelet is and when it should be served. I do hold to one rule, which you may adopt or discard as you please: I never serve an omelet for dessert if an omelet was the main course. I love omelets as much as anyone (except my mother), but I do try to keep a sense of perspective and moderation.

Sweet Omelet with Vanilla

Omelette sucrée à la vanille

This is a simple and easy dessert omelet and a fitting place to begin our exploration of sweet omelets. Because it cooks on the stove and employs an equal number of yolks and whites, this is not, strictly speaking, a soufflé omelet, but rather a mousseline omelet; most of the soufflé omelet recipes in this chapter can be adapted to this style. Unlike most French omelets, dessert omelets call for a little color, so it is okay, indeed, advisable to let them brown a little. I like to let the butter begin to brown, too, because it imparts a slightly nutty taste to the omelet.

Do use a very good vanilla—vanilla does all the work in this recipe and is vital to its success. For an especially elegant touch, surround the omelet with crème anglaise.

SERVES 1
Master Technique: French/Rolled

2 eggs, mixed
1 tablespoon vanilla extract
Seeds of 1 vanilla bean, husk reserved
1 tablespoon sugar
1 tablespoon unsalted butter
Mint sprig for garnish

Preheat a nonstick, 8- or 9-inch skillet over medium to medium-high heat.

Whisk the eggs, vanilla, vanilla bean seeds, and sugar with a fork until just combined.

Melt the butter in the skillet, swirl to coat the pan, and when the butter just begins to turn brown, pour the eggs into the pan.

Let the eggs sit undisturbed for about 5 seconds. With a fork or a spatula, move the eggs in a circular pattern, moving the eggs from the outside of the pan to the inside. At the same time, using sharp, short, and controlled motions, keep the skillet moving back and forth.

recipe continues . . .

Remove the pan from the heat and use the fork to "roll" the eggs from the far side of the pan to the side closest to you.

Grab underneath the handle of the pan with the palm of your hand, thumb on top of the handle, and invert the omelet, seam side down, onto a warm plate.

Garnish with a sprig of mint and the reserved vanilla bean husk.

....

Variations: I like to make this omelet with extract of almond, or with orange juice, and even with maple syrup. Maple syrup also makes a nice glaze under the broiler, but take care that it does not burn. A wonderful, spirited version of this omelet replaces the vanilla with a tablespoon of a sweet dessert wine and pairs it with a fine cheese on the side.

....

> **A TIP FROM MY MOTHER:** My mother liked to say that any recipe could be improved by doubling the amount of vanilla in it. It is not a bad rule, but I think it overwhelms this recipe.

Omelet with Almonds, Macaroons, and Black Currants

Omelette à la dijonnaise

This sweet omelet is one of the classics of French haute cuisine. Several versions abound, including one by Escoffier, but like this one (modeled on the recipe in *Larousse Gastronomique*), almost all of them call for a French custard layered between two thin, flat omelets flavored with almonds, macaroons, crème de cassis, topped with a simple meringue, and served with black currant jam.

The Dijon region of France, which gives its name to this dish, is highly regarded for its black currants, thus the name *à la dijonnaise*. Although many states banned black currants until very recently (some still do, because they are susceptible to disease), black currant jam is not difficult to find. Blackberries are not at all the same thing as black currants, but they will do as a substitute in this dish.

....

SERVES 3 TO 4
Master Technique: Frittata/Flat

2 eggs, mixed
½ cup plus 3 tablespoons granulated sugar
3 macaroons, crushed (I suggest coconut, but any sort will do)
1 tablespoon heavy cream
2 tablespoons unsalted butter, plus more for pan
¼ cup Crème pâtissière (recipe follows)
2 tablespoons ground almonds
1 tablespoon crème de cassis
4 egg whites
1 cup black currant or blackberry jam
Confectioners' sugar for dusting
Mint sprig to garnish

Mix together the eggs, 3 tablespoons of granulated sugar, macaroons, and heavy cream.

recipe continues . . .

Preheat an 8- or 9-inch skillet over medium heat.

Melt 1 tablespoon of the butter in the skillet, swirl to coat the pan, and when the butter sizzles, pour half of the egg mixture into the pan, and cook like a thin frittata. Remove the omelet from the pan and keep warm.

Repeat the process with the remaining butter and the egg mixture.

Remove the second omelet from the pan and keep warm.

Combine the pastry cream in a bowl with 1 tablespoon of the ground almonds and the crème de cassis.

Preheat the broiler.

Whip the egg whites to stiff peaks in a separate bowl, adding the remaining ½ cup of granulated sugar, 2 tablespoons at a time, to make a simple French meringue.

Place one of the flat omelets in a buttered ovenproof pan. Cover the omelet with the pastry cream, almonds, crème de cassis, and half of the black currant jam.

Place the second omelet on top of the custard, spread ¼ cup of pastry cream over the eggs, and cover completely with the egg whites. Dust the meringue with confectioners' sugar.

Glaze the meringue under the broiler. Remove from the oven and transfer to a warm serving platter. Surround the omelet with black currant jam, garnish with a sprig of mint, and serve warm.

Pastry Cream (Crème pâtissière)

This is a very basic recipe for pastry cream. You can flavor it with various liqueurs, coffee, or chocolate.

....

3 egg yolks

⅓ cup sugar

1 tablespoon all-purpose flour

1 tablespoon cornstarch

2 cups whole milk, warmed

1 vanilla bean, scraped and seeded

Whisk together the egg yolks, sugar, flour, and cornstarch.

In a saucepan, bring the milk, vanilla bean, and vanilla seeds to a simmer.

Remove the milk from the heat. Let the vanilla infuse the milk for about 10 minutes.

Slowly add the milk to the eggs, stirring constantly to prevent the mixture from scrambling.

Over a saucepan of simmering water (or a double boiler), heat the egg mixture, stirring briskly to keep the mixture from scrambling.

When the cream thickens (dip a wooden spoon into the cream and draw your finger across it. If the cream holds the line, it is done), remove it from the heat and strain into another bowl to remove the vanilla bean and seeds. Let cool, stirring frequently to keep it from clotting.

> **A TIP FROM MY MOTHER:** Let the milk cool until it is warm to the touch before adding it to the eggs.

Simple Omelet with Fresh Fruit

This recipe for an omelet with fresh fruit is another template for a nearly endless variety of omelets. I call for rhubarb here just because rhubarb is unloved, but almost any fruit will do, as would a basic fruit custard. This omelet is finished under the broiler. Many commercial kitchens used to have omelet irons, more commonly known as irons or salamanders, to finish sweet desserts. The red-hot iron was used to melt sugar on the top of a sweet omelet or any dish that called for a glaze of some sort. You can sometimes find them for sale now as "crème brûlée irons."

....

SERVES 2
Master Technique: American/Folded

4 eggs, mixed
1 tablespoon granulated sugar
Zest of 1 lemon
1 tablespoon water or sweet white dessert wine
1 tablespoon unsalted butter
¼ cup cooked chopped rhubarb, sweetened to taste
1 tablespoon confectioners' sugar (optional)
Whipped cream for garnish

Preheat a nonstick, 8- or 9-inch skillet over medium to medium-high heat.

Whisk the eggs, granulated sugar, lemon zest, and water or wine with a fork until just combined.

Melt the butter in the skillet, swirl to coat the pan, and when the butter just begins to brown, add the eggs. Swirl the eggs so they cover the entire bottom of the pan. Let the eggs sit quietly for about 10 seconds.

Holding the handle of the pan and using a spatula, pull the uncooked egg toward the center of the pan, proceeding calmly and deliberately around the compass, north to south to east to west. Use a spatula to lift the eggs from the rim of the pan, and move the remaining uncooked egg under the cooked portion.

Let the omelet cook for a minute or two, occasionally moving the uncooked egg under the cooked portion as necessary.

When the eggs have set, add the rhubarb to center of the eggs, and then, using a spatula, fold the omelet in half, moving from the outside of the pan to the inside.

If you like, dust the top of the omelet with confectioners' sugar and glaze under the broiler.

Turn out the omelet onto a warm plate. Serve with whipped cream.

Soufflé Omelet with Liqueur

This is another easy dessert, but in the form of a traditional soufflé omelet. It is delicious just as it is, but it also works as a sound foundation for more elaborate dishes. If you cook it on the stovetop, this omelet will take well to a flambé. Add a tablespoon or two of your favorite liqueur to the pan and flame just before serving.

SERVES 2
Master Technique: Soufflé

2 eggs, separated
1 tablespoon Crème de Mûre (or another liqueur to your taste)
1 teaspoon cream of tartar
1 tablespoon sugar
Pinch of salt
1 tablespoon unsalted butter
Fresh blackberries for garnish

Preheat the oven to 350°F.

Preheat an ovenproof 8- or 9-inch skillet over medium heat.

Stir the egg yolks with a whisk until they are light and pale. Whisk in the liqueur.

Whip the egg whites in a separate bowl with the cream of tartar, sugar, and salt until soft peaks form. Gently fold the whites into the yolks.

Melt the butter in the skillet, swirl to coat the pan, and when the butter bubbles and sizzles but is not smoking or brown, pour the eggs into the pan.

Let the eggs sit quietly for about 2 minutes. Gently run a spatula around the edges of the omelet to make sure it is not sticking, and then place the omelet in the oven.

Bake the omelet for 4 to 5 minutes. The omelet is finished when the top of the eggs have set and are spongy.

Invert the omelet onto a warm plate so the browned side is visible and garnish with fresh blackberries (or whatever fruit is in your liqueur), and serve immediately.

Variation: Some older recipes for sweet soufflé omelets suggest incorporating a tablespoon or two of whipped cream into the egg whites.

The Way to Flambé an Omelet

A flambé, like dessert, is more extravagance than necessity, but cooking is as much theater as technique, as even a source as commanding as the *Larousse Gastronomique* recognizes. Plus, it's fun to flambé and there is not much risk involved. Well, not too much, anyway, but there are some things to keep in mind.

The most important thing to know is that you should never add alcohol to the pan straight from the bottle. The reason is plain: If the flame should reach too high, you don't want to feed it with more alcohol or, worse, have the flame ignite the bottle.

The same logic counsels three more precautions. First, it is best to take the pan off the heat when you add the alcohol. Second, always flambé in moderation. In most dishes, you need only 2 or 3 tablespoons of alcohol to achieve the proper effect. Third, have nearby a lid big enough to cover the pan should the flame get too high.

Precautions in place, the way to flambé is simple.

Some folks will counsel you to warm the alcohol in a saucepan. This is not needed, but if your alcohol has been chilled, bring it to room temperature.

Once the alcohol has joined the eggs in the pan, light it. It is important that you do this with a sense of confidence and flair, but also safely. A match or a lighter is safest; although you will see more adventuresome (that sounds nicer than foolhardy) chefs tilt the pan over a gas burner to set things alight. Shake the pan gently while the alcohol burns.

How long should you flambé your omelet? When the fire subsides, stop. The flame should expire very quickly—there is not very much alcohol to burn.

Finally, there is one last, oft-neglected, but crucial question: *Where* should you flambé? The answer is that you must flambé where your guests can watch the show. What is the point, otherwise? If you are the cautious sort, you might also choose somewhere near a phone so your guests can call 911.

If you do a lot of entertaining, or are thinking of opening an omelet restaurant, consider investing in a *table à flamber*, or a flambé trolley, sometimes called a gueridon. A flambé trolley is a small cart equipped with burners and wheels that moves from table to table, just so the chef can dazzle the diner. You can find several suppliers online. The one I want is on sale for just over $7,000.

Simple Jam Omelet with Fruit

Jams and jellies make for an endless variety of dessert (or breakfast) omelets. They are simple and quick to make, but if you purchase one, do take care to use a high-quality jam or preserve. Taste the jam before you use it—the sweetness of jams and jellies can vary considerably depending upon the fruit and the manufacturer. This very traditional recipe couples the jam with fresh fruit. I like to garnish jam omelets with crushed macaroons and a fruit coulis or a fruit sauce.

....

SERVES 1

Master Technique: American/Folded

½ cup roughly chopped fresh or dried apricots
½ cup apricot jam
1 teaspoon fresh lemon zest
2 eggs, mixed
2 tablespoons sugar
1 tablespoon water or sweet white dessert wine
2 tablespoons unsalted butter
Sauce à l'orange for garnish (optional, recipe follows)
Crushed macaroons for garnish

Combine the apricots with ¼ cup of the apricot jam and the lemon zest. Let them marinate in the apricot jam for about 30 minutes. I find it helpful to warm the apricots and the jam over a very gentle flame for a couple of minutes.

Preheat a nonstick, 8- or 9-inch skillet over medium to medium-high heat.

Whisk the eggs, sugar, and water or wine with a fork until just combined.

Melt the butter in the skillet, swirl to coat the pan, and when the butter just begins to turn brown, pour the eggs into the pan.

Let the eggs sit quietly for about 10 seconds. Then, holding the handle of the pan and using a spatula, pull the uncooked egg toward the center of the pan, proceeding calmly and deliberately around the compass, north to south and east to west. Use a spatula to lift the eggs from the rim of the pan, and move the remaining uncooked egg under the cooked portion.

When the bottom of the eggs begin to set, lower the heat to medium-low and let the omelet cook until the eggs cook through and the bottom of the omelet turns a light or golden brown, about 3 to 4 minutes. If the top of the eggs seem not to finish, you can speed things along by covering the pan with a lid for about 1 minute.

If you like, you can fold the omelet in half, as if an American omelet, or you can serve it open-faced.

Turn out the omelet onto a warm plate. Spoon the remaining ¼ cup of apricot jam around the omelet or serve with a Sauce à l'orange. If the jam is too thick, thin it with a little white wine or fresh lemon juice. Garnish with macaroons.

Variations: Please use whatever jam or jelly suits your fancy. Preserved and candied fruits work very well in this recipe too.

Sauce à l'orange

This sauce is based on a Pierre Franey recipe.

1 cup apricot preserves
½ cup water
½ cup chopped orange slices
Zest of 1 orange
Zest of 1 lemon
1 tablespoon Grand Marnier

Combine the apricot preserves and water in a small saucepan. Stir over low heat until smooth.

Add the chopped orange, orange zest, lemon zest, and Grand Marnier. Stir until combined. Serve warm.

Soufflé Omelet with Pears and Pecans

This attractive dish works best with caramelized pears, but poached pears will also do nicely. Pears pair well with a flambé.

....

SERVES 1

Master Technique: Soufflé

1 medium pear (about 6 ounces), peeled, cored, and sliced
3 tablespoons unsalted butter
2 tablespoons sugar
1 ½ cups chopped pecans, plus more for garnish
2 eggs, separated
1 tablespoon Poire Williams
1 teaspoon cream of tartar
Pinch of salt
Whipped cream for garnish

Sauté the pears in 2 tablespoons of the butter and 1 tablespoon of the sugar in a medium skillet over medium heat until the pears are tender and begin to brown. Add the pecans and stir gently to make sure they are coated with the butter and sugar.

Stir the egg yolks with a whisk until they are light and pale. Add the Poire Williams.

Whip the egg whites in a separate bowl with the cream of tartar, remaining tablespoon of sugar, and the salt until soft peaks form.

Gently fold the whites into the yolks.

Preheat a nonstick, 8- or 9-inch skillet over medium to medium-high heat.

Melt the remaining tablespoon of butter in the skillet, swirl to coat the pan, and when the butter bubbles and sizzles, pour the eggs into the pan.

Let the eggs sit quietly for about 10 seconds. Then, grabbing the handle of the pan and using a spatula, stir the eggs in the pan. At the same time, using crisp, short motions, keep the skillet moving back and forth.

When the bottom of the eggs begin to set, lower the heat to medium-low and let the omelet cook until the eggs cook through and when the bottom of the omelet turns a light or golden brown, about 3 to 4 minutes. If the top of the eggs seem not to finish, you can speed things along by covering the pan with a lid for about 1 minute.

Spread the pears and pecans over the omelet, reserving a few slices of pears and nuts for garnish.

If you like, you can fold the omelet in half, as if an American omelet, or you can serve it open-faced.

Turn out the omelet onto a plate, garnish with the reserved pear slices and whipped cream. Serve immediately.

Variation: Instead of pears and pecans, try plums and almonds.

Sweet Omelet with Candied Walnuts

This very unusual omelet is one of my favorites, especially for holiday meals, which for some reason is the only time I sugar nuts. Sugaring is very simple and I urge you to try it, whether or not a holiday is in close sight.

....

SERVES 1
Master Recipe: Soufflé

2 cups whole walnuts, plus more for garnish
1 cup plus 1 tablespoon sugar
2 tablespoons unsalted butter
2 eggs, separated
1 tablespoon Cointreau (or another liqueur to your taste)
1 teaspoon cream of tartar
Pinch of salt
Whipped cream for garnish

Toast the walnuts in a large, dry skillet over medium heat for about 10 minutes.

Add ½ cup of the sugar and 1 tablespoon of the butter to the nuts in the frying pan. Cook the nuts until the sugar begins to melt and starts to turn golden. Remove from the heat immediately and stir gently to make sure all the nuts are coated with the sugar and butter.

Dry the walnuts on a baking sheet covered with parchment. Separate the nuts from one another and allow to cool completely.

Stir the egg yolks with a whisk until they are light and pale. Add the Cointreau and 1 tablespoon of sugar.

Whip the egg whites in a separate bowl with the cream of tartar, the remaining ½ cup of the sugar, and the salt until soft peaks form.

Gently fold the whites into the yolks.

Preheat a nonstick, 8- or 9-inch skillet over medium to medium-high heat.

Melt the remaining tablespoon of butter in the skillet, swirl to coat the pan, and when the butter bubbles and sizzles, pour the eggs into the pan.

Let the eggs sit quietly for about 10 seconds. Then, grabbing the handle of the pan and using a spatula, stir the eggs in the pan. At the same time, using crisp, short motions, keep the skillet moving back and forth.

When the bottom of the eggs begin to set, lower the heat to medium-low and let the omelet cook until the eggs cook through and when the bottom of the omelet turns a light or golden brown, about 3 to 4 minutes. If the top of the eggs seem not to finish, you can speed things along by covering the pan with a lid for about 1 minute.

Spread the walnuts over the omelet, reserving a few for garnish.

If you like, you can fold the omelet in half, as if an American omelet, or you can serve it open-faced.

Turn out the omelet onto a plate, garnish with the reserved walnuts and whipped cream. Serve immediately.

Variations: Pecans (especially with a tablespoon of pecan-flavored liqueur) or almonds would make a fine substitute for walnuts. I would avoid peanuts, but it is your omelet.

Sweet Omelet with Sugared Strawberries

Sweet Omelet Pompadour

This is a much less intricate, and to my mind a much improved, version of an Omelette surprise Pompadour, not least because it has no surprises in it. It is delicious just with strawberries, but sugaring and macerating the berries gives them additional flavor and renders a simple but elegant sauce, worthy of a state dinner.

....

SERVES 2
Master Technique: Soufflé

1 cup hulled and sliced fresh strawberries
3 tablespoons granulated sugar
1 teaspoon fresh lemon juice
2 tablespoons strawberry liqueur or Grand Marnier
1 to 2 teaspoons all-purpose flour (optional)
3 eggs, separated
1 teaspoon balsamic vinegar
Pinch of salt
1 tablespoon unsalted butter
Mint sprig for garnish
Fanned strawberry for garnish (optional)
1 tablespoon crème fraîche for garnish (optional)

Place the strawberries in a large bowl. Sprinkle with 2 tablespoons of the sugar and the lemon juice and liqueur. Let the strawberries sit for about 15 minutes.

Drain the strawberries, reserving the liquid. If the liquid is very thin, add a little flour to make a sauce or drizzle.

Preheat a nonstick, 8- or 9-inch skillet over medium to medium-high heat.

Whisk the egg yolks and balsamic vinegar with a fork until just combined.

Whip the egg whites in a separate bowl with the remaining sugar and the salt until soft peaks form.

Gently fold the whites into the yolks.

Preheat a nonstick, 8- or 9-inch skillet over medium to medium-high heat.

Melt the butter in the skillet, swirl to coat the pan, and when the butter bubbles and sizzles, pour the eggs into the pan.

Let the eggs sit quietly for about 10 seconds. Then, grabbing the handle of the pan and using a spatula, stir the eggs in the pan. At the same time, using crisp, short motions, keep the skillet moving back and forth.

When the bottom of the eggs begin to set, lower the heat to medium-low and let the omelet cook until the eggs cook through and when the bottom of the omelet turns a light or golden brown, about 3 to 4 minutes. If the top of the eggs seem not to finish, you can speed things along by covering the pan with a lid for about 1 minute.

Spread the strawberries over the omelet, reserving a few for garnish.

If you like, you can fold the omelet in half, as if an American omelet, or you can serve it open-faced.

Turn out the omelet onto a plate. Drizzle with the reserved strawberry-liqueur sauce and garnish with mint and a fanned strawberry or a dollop of crème fraîche.

....

Variations: Almost any fruit, if macerated, will release juices that you can use to make a quick sauce. In the same way, if you are using canned fruit, save the juice, sweeten it if necessary, and reduce in a saucepan. In place of strawberries, use whatever berries are fresh and in season—blueberries work especially well. I also like to make this omelet with sugared cranberries, and sometimes with dried cranberries. .

....

Coffee Soufflé Omelet

If you like coffee with dessert, this omelet will become a favorite. I like it because it is not too sweet. It goes great with a double espresso or, if you prefer, a coffee with a splash of something spirituous. You might add a splash of a complementary liqueur, such as amaretto, Kahlúa, Frangelico, Baileys, or Grand Marnier. For something a little more elegant, make a Coffee and Almond Soufflé Omelet by adding finely ground almonds and ¼ teaspoon of almond extract to the egg whites.

Serves 1
Master Technique: Soufflé

2 eggs, separated
2 tablespoons sugar
2 tablespoons very strong brewed coffee, cold
1 teaspoon cream of tartar
Pinch of salt
1 tablespoon unsalted butter
Mint sprig for garnish
1 tablespoon chocolate-covered coffee beans for garnish
Crème anglaise for garnish (optional)

Preheat the oven to 350°F.

Stir the egg yolks with 1 tablespoon of the sugar with a whisk until they are light and pale. Add the coffee to the yolks and mix thoroughly.

Whip the egg whites in a separate bowl with the cream of tartar, 1 tablespoon of the sugar, and the salt until soft peaks form.

Gently fold the whites into the yolks.

Preheat a nonstick, ovenproof 8- or 9-inch skillet over medium to medium-high heat.

Melt the butter in the skillet, swirl to coat the pan, and when the butter just begins to brown, add the eggs. Swirl the eggs so they cover the entire bottom of the pan.

Cook over medium to medium-low heat, until the eggs set, about 1 minute.

Transfer to the oven and bake until the omelet fluffs and turns golden brown—perhaps 5 or 6 minutes. The soufflé is done when the top of the omelet feels spongy to your finger.

Fold the omelet in half and turn it onto a plate. Garnish with a sprig of mint and chocolate coffee beans. For an especially elegant touch, surround the omelet with crème anglaise.

Chocolate Soufflé Omelet

I love chocolate omelets because so many people seem so startled by the idea. A chocolate omelet might seem odd, but eggs take beautifully to chocolate, as anyone who has ever had a chocolate cake or a chocolate pudding or a chocolate mousse or a chocolate custard—or a chocolate soufflé—knows. This recipe incorporates melted chocolate into the yolks, giving the omelet a beautiful dark complexion. Making it in the oven gives it a light, almost cakelike texture.

SERVES 1 TO 2
Master Technique: Soufflé

2 eggs, separated
3 tablespoons granulated sugar
3 ounces bittersweet or semisweet chocolate (such as Guittard, Perugina, or Valhrona), melted and cooled
1 teaspoon hazelnut liqueur (optional)
1 teaspoon cream of tartar
Pinch of salt
1 tablespoon unsalted butter
Confectioners' sugar for sprinkling (optional)
Fresh raspberries for garnish (optional)
Mint sprig for garnish (optional)
Chocolate sauce for garnish (optional)

Preheat the oven to 350°F.

Stir the egg yolks and 1 tablespoon of the granulated sugar with a whisk until they are light and pale. Add the melted chocolate and the hazelnut extract, if using, to the yolks and mix thoroughly.

Whip the egg whites in a separate bowl with the cream of tartar, 2 tablespoons of the granulated sugar, and the salt until soft peaks form.

Gently fold the whites into the yolks.

Preheat a nonstick, ovenproof 8- or 9-inch skillet over medium heat.

Melt the butter in the skillet, swirl to coat the pan, and when the butter bubbles and sizzles but is not smoking or brown, pour the eggs into the pan.

Let the eggs sit quietly for about 2 minutes. Gently run a spatula around the edges of the omelet to make sure it is not sticking, and then place the omelet in the oven.

Bake the omelet for about 8 to 9 minutes. The omelet is finished when the top of the eggs have set and are spongy.

Using a spatula, gently fold the omelet in half, moving from the outside of the pan to the inside.

Turn out the omelet onto a plate. I like to sprinkle confectioners' sugar over the top of the omelet and to garnish it with a few raspberries or a sprig of mint. You might also serve it with a simple chocolate sauce.

Variations: Many recipes for chocolate omelets are just a simple omelette sucrée covered with chocolate sauce. These are delicious, too. The trick is not to drown the omelet in the sauce. Almonds are a wonderful addition to this omelet. For a Chocolate Soufflé Omelet with Almonds, add almond extract to the yolks and finely ground almonds to the whipped egg whites.

Chocolate and a
Shot (or Two) Omelet

Chocolate and Espresso Omelet

Any recipe that calls for coffee is better with espresso.

....

SERVES 2
Master Technique: Soufflé

2 eggs, separated
3 tablespoons granulated sugar
3 ounces bittersweet or semisweet chocolate (such as Guittard, Perugina, or
    Valhrona), melted and cooled
2 tablespoons brewed espresso coffee, cooled
1 teaspoon cream of tartar
Pinch of salt
1 tablespoon unsalted butter
Confectioners' sugar for garnish
Chocolate-espresso sauce for garnish (optional)
1 tablespoon chocolate-covered coffee beans for garnish (optional)
Raspberry Coulis (optional; recipe follows)

Preheat the oven to 350°F.

Stir the egg yolks and 1 tablespoon of the granulated sugar with a whisk until they are light and pale. Add the chocolate and the espresso to the yolks and mix thoroughly.

Whip the egg whites in a separate bowl with the cream of tartar, 2 tablespoons of the granulated sugar, and the salt until soft peaks form.

Gently fold the whites into the yolks.

Preheat a nonstick, ovenproof 8- or 9-inch skillet over medium heat.

Melt the butter in the skillet, swirl to coat the pan, and when the butter bubbles and sizzles but is not smoking or brown, pour the eggs into the pan.

Let the eggs sit quietly for about 2 minutes. Gently run a spatula around the edges of the omelet to make sure it is not sticking, and then place the omelet in the oven.

Bake the omelet for about 8 or 9 minutes. The omelet is finished when the top of the eggs have set and are spongy.

Turn out the omelet onto a plate. Drizzle the omelet with a chocolate-espresso sauce or raspberry coulis and sprinkle with confectioners' sugar and chocolate-covered coffee beans.

Raspberry Coulis

A fresh fruit coulis is something between a sauce and a garnish and should be a staple in every cook's repertoire. A coulis adds both flavor and color to a dessert and, if you have any artistic talent at all (I do not), can be used to paint a plate in almost any pattern. This recipe is very basic—you can change it up by adding various fruit juices, extracts, liqueurs, and zests. Even frozen fruits will do.

1 pint fresh raspberries (about 2 cups)
1 teaspoon fresh lemon juice (optional)
Sugar

Puree the fruit and lemon juice in a food processor. Taste and add sugar, as necessary.

Strain the fruit in a fine-mesh strainer or colander to remove the seeds.

Funnel the puree into a ketchup bottle or a pastry bag and refrigerate until using.

Friar's Omelet

The inspiration for this recipe is an old Scottish dish traditionally made with buttered bread crumbs and Bramley apples (you may substitute any sour or cooking apple) or rhubarb. The older recipes layer the apples over the bread crumbs, stir in a couple of eggs, and bake it all in the oven. My version resembles a sweet frittata.

....

SERVES 2 TO 3
Master Technique: Flat/Frittata

3 cups cored and thinly sliced apple
3 to 4 tablespoons unsalted butter
3 tablespoons granulated sugar
½ teaspoon freshly grated nutmeg
1 teaspoon ground cinnamon (optional)
1 cup (about 2 ounces) buttered bread crumbs or small croutons
6 eggs, mixed
1 tablespoon water
Confectioners' sugar for sprinkling (optional)

Preheat the oven to 350°F.

Sauté the apple slices in 2 tablespoons of the butter in an ovenproof 10- to 12-inch skillet over medium heat until tender. Add the granulated sugar, nutmeg, and cinnamon, if using. (Cinnamon gives the apples more of an apple pie taste. I prefer this omelet without it.)

Add the buttered bread crumbs to the apples.

Whisk the eggs and water with a fork until just combined.

If necessary, add a tablespoon or two of butter to the apples and bread crumbs. When the butter sizzles, add the eggs to the pan. Cook over low heat until the eggs set, about 3 to 5 minutes. If there is uncooked egg, lift an edge up and tilt the pan so the uncooked egg runs underneath the cooked egg.

After the edges of the egg begin to set, loosen them gently with a spatula, and then put the pan into the oven for approximately 12 to 15 minutes.

Let the omelet sit for about 10 minutes before slicing and serving. I like to dust the omelet with a little confectioners' sugar.

Variations: Traditional recipes often call for "rusk" instead of bread crumbs. Rusk is a very old-fashioned dish of biscuit or bread, usually baked twice to make the biscuit very hard and dense. It is not the same, but you might try zwieback or Melba toast, or even biscotti, as a substitute.

Flambéed Apple and Plum Omelet
Omelette aux pommes et quetsches flambées

This is an elegant and very traditional omelet from Southwest France. I use apples and plums because that is how I first came across this dish in a small restaurant just outside of Sarlat a few years ago, but any fresh fruit would work as well.

....

SERVES 2
Master Technique: Soufflé

1 cup cored and thinly sliced apple
1 cup thinly sliced plum
4 tablespoons unsalted butter
4 tablespoons granulated sugar
3 tablespoons Armagnac or rum (or similar liqueur)
4 eggs, separated
1 teaspoon cream of tartar
Pinch of salt
Confectioners' sugar for sprinkling
Mint sprig for garnish

Sauté the apples and plums in 2 tablespoons of the butter and 3 tablespoons of the granulated sugar over medium heat until they are tender and the apples begin to caramelize. Add 2 tablespoons of the Armagnac and flambé the fruits.

Remove the pan from the heat and strain the fruits, reserving the juices. If necessary, reduce the juices to about ¼ cup.

Stir the egg yolks with a whisk until they are light and pale. Whisk in the remaining tablespoon of Armagnac.

Whip the egg whites in a separate bowl with the cream of tartar, remaining 2 tablespoons of granulated sugar, and the salt until soft peaks form.

Gently fold the whites into the yolks.

Preheat a nonstick, 8- or 9-inch skillet over medium to medium-high heat.

Melt the remaining 2 tablespoons of butter in the skillet, swirl to coat the pan, and when the butter bubbles and sizzles but is not smoking or brown, pour the eggs into the pan.

Let the eggs sit quietly for about 10 seconds. Then, grabbing the handle of the pan and using a spatula, stir the eggs in the pan. At the same time, using crisp, short motions, keep the skillet moving back and forth.

When the bottom of the eggs begin to set, lower the heat to medium-low and let the omelet cook until the eggs cook through and the bottom of the omelet turns a light or golden brown, about 3 to 4 minutes. If the top of the eggs seem not to finish, you can speed things along by covering the pan with a lid for about 1 minute.

Place the sautéed fruits in the center of the eggs.

Using a spatula, gently fold the omelet in half, moving from the outside of the pan to the inside. If you prefer, you can serve this omelet open faced.

Turn out the omelet onto a plate and spoon the reserved fruit juices over and around the omelet. Dust with confectioners' sugar, garnish with mint, and serve immediately.

....

Variations: One of the riches of classical French cuisine is the delightful combination of prunes and Armagnac. In this recipe, I would first soak the prunes in Armagnac for an hour or two.

You can also finish this omelet in the oven, as does Paula Wolfert in her recipe for a Soufflé Omelet with Fresh Fruits in the wonderful cookbook, *The Cooking of Southwest France.* Wolfert starts the omelet on the stovetop and finishes it in the oven at 425°F for about 5 minutes. Dust the omelet with confectioners' sugar.

....

Sweet Omelet with Rum Sauce

Omelet au rhum

This is my favorite omelet, so I have saved it for last. I like it more than I like my wife, more than I like my kids, and almost as much as I like my dog. It is also one of the oldest of dessert omelets, simple to make and spectacular to serve.

....

SERVES 2

Master Technique: Soufflé

2 eggs, separated
3 to 4 tablespoons rum
1 teaspoon cream of tartar
1 tablespoon plus 1 teaspoon sugar
Pinch of salt
1 tablespoon unsalted butter
Rum Sauce (recipe follows)

Stir the egg yolks with a whisk until they are light and pale. Whisk in 1 to 2 tablespoons of the rum.

Whip the egg whites in a separate bowl with the cream of tartar, 1 tablespoon of the sugar, and the salt until soft peaks form.

Gently fold the whites into the yolks.

Preheat a nonstick, 8- or 9-inch skillet over medium to medium-high heat.

Melt the butter in the skillet, swirl to coat the pan, and when the butter bubbles and sizzles but is not smoking or brown, pour the eggs into the pan.

Let the eggs sit quietly for about 10 seconds. Then, grabbing the handle of the pan and using a spatula, stir the eggs in the pan. At the same time, using crisp, short motions, keep the skillet moving back and forth.

When the bottom of the eggs begin to set, lower the heat to medium-low and let the omelet cook until the eggs cook through and the bottom of the omelet turns a light or golden brown, about 3 to 4 minutes. If the top of the eggs seem not to finish, you can speed things along by covering the pan with a lid for about 1 minute.

Using a spatula, gently fold the omelet in half, moving from the outside of the pan to the inside. Sprinkle the omelet with the remaining teaspoon of sugar and an additional tablespoon or two of rum to flambé, if desired.

Turn out the omelet onto a plate. Spoon the rum sauce over the top of the omelet. Serve immediately.

Variations: In place of the rum, try a nice sherry, perhaps an amontillado, or for something very different, limoncello accompanied by grilled lemons.

It is wildly untraditional, but crushed Butter Rum Lifesavers candy make the best garnish for this omelet.

Rum Sauce

¼ cup light brown sugar
¼ cup unsalted butter
⅓ cup heavy cream
3 tablespoons rum

Place all the ingredients in a medium saucepan over medium-high heat.

Bring the sauce to a gentle boil and let cook for about 3 minutes, stirring constantly to prevent scorching.

A TIP FROM MY MOTHER: Do you remember my mother's rule of thumb about vanilla? It works better for rum.

Acknowledgments

———◦┃◉┃◦———

I owe a debt I am eager to acknowledge but greater than I can square to all of my teachers, both in the classroom and the kitchen. Four folks in particular deserve a special word and may never know, so . . . thank you, John Colby Myer, late of the late Nasson College; Peter Poor, also of Nasson; and Dan Cole and Margaret Garrison, both formerly of Seattle Prep. Thank you as well to the many colleagues, students, and friends at Wesleyan University who helped me test recipes.

I am grateful to coffee shop companions in Maine and Connecticut for their encouragement and counsel. These include, I am happy to say by name, Jay Carter, Chris Rossetti, and Tom Royle. *Thanks* is too plain and *tribute* too formal a word for Jane Miller, friend and logophile. Thank you as well to Joan Nagy, of the Simsbury, Connecticut Public Library, and Kristi Bryant, of the Wells, Maine Public Library.

My thanks as well to Dottie and John Turi, for pretty much everything.

I am especially grateful for words of support and encouragement from Darra Goldstein (friend, colleague, inspiration, and among the very first to see an idea for a book here), Molly O'Neill, and my untiring agent, Angela Miller. A special thanks also to Chi-Hoon Kim and Kate McCrery, for their boundless enthusiasm and encouragement of many years, and to Diane Wright, for the lovely illustrations.

The good folks at The Countryman Press, including Ann Treistman, Sarah Bennett, and Aurora Bell, deserve more than a quick note here, and I am very grateful for their enthusiasm and hard work.

Finally, I owe a debt greater than I can even acknowledge to Linda, Alex, and Ellery. Their influence shows in every word in this book, and in a whole lot of other words that are not.

Bibliography

Beard, James. *American Cookery.* New York: Little, Brown, 2009.

Chamberlain, Narcissa G. *The Omelette Book.* Boston: David R. Godine, 1955.

Davidson, Alan. *Oxford Companion to Food.* New York: Oxford University Press, 1999.

de Lyon, Madame Romaine. *The Art of Cooking Omelettes.* New York: Doubleday, 1963.

Escoffier, Auguste. *The Escoffier Cookbook: A Guide to the Fine Art of French Cuisine.* New York: Crown Publishers, 1969.

Lallemand, Roger. *Les Omelettes.* Marseilles: Jean Laffitte, 1986.

Meyer, Adolphe. *Eggs in a Thousand Ways: A Guide for the Preparation of Eggs for the Table.* New York: Hotel Monthly Press, 1917.

Ruhlman, Michael. *Egg: A Culinary Exploration of the World's Most Versatile Ingredient.* New York: Little, Brown and Company, 2014.

Toops, Diane. *Eggs: A Global History.* London: Reaktion Books, 2014.

Toussaint-Samat, Maguelonne. *A History of Food*, revised ed. Translated by Anthea Bell. New York: Wiley-Blackwell, 2009.

Wheaton, Barbara Ketcham. *Savoring the Past: The French Kitchen and Table from 1300 to 1789.* New York: Simon & Schuster, 1983.

Wildgen, Michelle. "Ode to an Egg," *Tin House Magazine,* 2004.

Notes

13   *philosophy did not consist* . . . Pierre Hadot, *Philosophy as a Way of Life: Spiritual Exercises from Socrates to Foucault* (New York: Wiley, 1995), 82–83.

13   *philosopher's stone* . . . Diane Toops, *Eggs: A Global History* (London: Reaktion Books, 2014), 7. Surely, there is also something of philosophical significance in the fact that Ludwig Wittgenstein found a single egg sufficient for dinner. Steven Shapin, "The Philosopher and the Chicken: On the Dietetics of Disembodied Knowledge," in *Science Incarnate: Historical Embodiments of Natural Knowledge*, ed. Christopher Lawrence and Steven Shapin (Chicago: University of Chicago Press, 1998).

13   *as Ezra Pound* . . . Ezra Pound, "Statement of Being," poemhunter.com/poem/statement-of-being/.

14   *is the transforming* . . . Robert Rowland Smith, *Breakfast with Socrates* (Boston: Free Press, 2009), 169.

14   *Omelets Revisited* . . . [etc.]: Stephanie Lyness, "Omelets Revisited," *Cook's Illustrated*, September/October 1993, 21.

14   *about 80 strokes*: "Perfect French Omelets," *America's Test Kitchen: Best-Ever Recipes*, 2013, p. 72, https://www.cooksillustrated.com/recipes/4594-perfect-french-omelets

14   *Kitchen Performance Anxiety* . . . J. Mulkerrins, "Focus," *Sunday Times* (London), December 16, 2001, 19. See also James Chapman, "Nigella and Kitchen Performance Anxiety," *Daily Mail*, dailymail.co.uk/news/article-89910/Nigella-kitchen-performance-anxiety.html.

15   *spoilt idiot-child* . . . M. F. K. Fisher, "The Anatomy of the Recipe," in *With Bold Knife and Fork* (London: Chatto and Windis, 1983), 17.

15   *kind of incivility* . . . [etc.]: Joanne Finkelstein, *Dining Out: A Sociology of Modern Manners* (New York: New York University Press, 1989), 174.

15   *someone else's set* . . . [etc.]: Janet Floyd and Laurel Foster, eds., *The Recipe Reader: Narratives—Contexts—Traditions* (Burlington, VT: Ashgate, 2003), 3.

15   *undoubtedly the finest* . . . Auguste Escoffier, *The Escoffier Cookbook: A Guide to the Fine Art of French Cuisine* (New York: Crown Publishers, 1969), 180.

16   *the word 'difficult'* . . . [etc.]: John Ciardi, *How Does a Poem Mean?* www.csun.edu/~krowlands/Content/Academic_Resources/Poetry_Instruction/ciardi.pdf.

16   *mistakes are delicious*: Michael Ruhlman, *Egg: A Culinary Exploration of the World's Most Versatile Ingredient* (New York: Little, Brown and Company, 2014), 61.

16   *Omelet* mécanique: With apologies to John Thorne, *Outlaw Cook* (Berkeley, CA: Northpoint Press, 1994).

17   *By his own* . . . Pierre Franey, *More 60-Minute Gourmet* (New York: Fawcett, 1981), 86.

18   *"perfect"*: I consider the meaning and implications of perfect recipes, especially for civic life, in John E. Finn, "The Perfect Recipe: Taste and Tyranny, Cooks and Citizens," *Food, Culture, and Society* 14, no. 4 (2011), 503–24.

18   *the world is awash* . . . Ruhlman, *Egg*, xiii.

18   *matter of authentic* . . . Lisa Heldke, *Exotic Appetites: Ruminations of a Food Adventurer* (New York: Routledge, 2003), 113.

18   *only by certain* . . . For a discussion, see Michael Steinberger, "Can Anyone Save French Food,"

New York Times, March 28, 2014, nytimes.com/2014/03/30/magazine/can-anyone-save
-french-food.html?_r=0; see also Steve Denning, "Authenticity and Italian Food," May
21, 2004, stevedenning.com/Storytelling-in-the-News/156-authenticity-and-italian
-food.aspx.

18   *Is anything about . . .* Carolyn Korsmeyer, *Making Sense of Taste: Food and Philosophy* (Ithaca, NY: Cornell University Press, 2002), 86.

18   *as Proust . . .* Marcel Proust, *Remembrance of Things Past* (New York: Vintage, 1982); see also David E. Sutton, *Remembrance of Repasts: An Anthropology of Food and Memory* (Oxford: Berg Press, 2001).

19   *It was the perfect . . .* Mark Bittman, "Perfect French Omelets," February 16, 2009, thebittenword
.typepad.com/thebittenword/2009/02/perfect-french-omelets.html.

19   *Charles Dicken's Bitzer . . .* Charles Dickens, *Hard Times* (London: Bradbury and Evans, 1854).
"Bitzer," said Thomas Gradgrind, "your definition of a horse." "Quadruped. Gramnivorous. Forty teeth, namely twenty-four grinders, four eye-teeth, and twelve incisive. Sheds coat in the spring; in marshy countries sheds hoofs too. Hoofs hard, but requiring to be shod with iron. Age known by marks in mouth." Thus (and much more) Bitzer. "Now girl number twenty," said Mr. Gradgrind, "you know what a horse is."

19   *Cookbooks should . . .* Daniel Patterson, "Do Recipes Make You a Better Cook?" 2007, foodandwine
.com/articles/do-recipes-make-you-a-better-cook.

20   *perfect one . . .* Narcissa G. Chamberlain, *The Omelette Book* (Boston: David R. Godine, Publisher, Inc., 2009), preface.

20   *there is only . . .* Elizabeth David, *An Omelette and a Glass of Wine* (London: Grub Street, 2009).

20   *Platonic ideal . . .* [etc.]: Marilyn Hacker, "Omelette," *A Stranger's Mirror: New and Selected Poems 1994–2014* (New York: W. W. Norton, 2015), 175.

20   *in their essence . . .* Marie Simmons, *The Good Egg: More than 200 Fresh Approaches from Breakfast to Dessert* (New York: Houghton Mifflin, 2000), 39.

20   *is a little like . . .* Madame Romaine de Lyon, *The Art of Cooking Omelettes* (New York: Doubleday, 1963), 40.

20   *expresses the meaninglessness . . .* Please consult this truly wonderful website: Marty Davis, "The Jean-Paul Sartre Cookbook," pvspade.com/Sartre/cookbook.html.

21   *essentially contested concept*: This is something of a simplification of Gallie's work, but it is a common one. See W. B. Gallie, "Essentially Contested Concepts," in *Proceedings of the Aristotelian Society* 56 (1955–56), 167–98.

21   *There are those . . .* This would be, for example, the generous reading of such cookbooks as Rick Bayless, *Authentic Mexican: Regional Cooking from the Heart of Mexico* (New York: William Morrow, 1987).

21   *European Union granted . . .* "The TSG label, which was created in 1992, stipulates that a product has to conform to traditional ingredients and cooking methods but does not have to be made in a specific geographic area." Nick Squires, "Neapolitan Pizza Wins Official Protection from EU," June 2009, telegraph.co.uk/foodanddrink/6771819/Neapolitan-pizza-wins
-official-protection-from-EU
.html. (For a more extensive discussion, see Finn, "The Perfect Recipe.")

22   *the ambiguity . . .* Joan P. Alcock, "The Ambiguity of Authenticity," in *Authenticity in the Kitchen: Proceedings of the Oxford Symposium on Food and Cookery*, ed. Richard Hosking (London: Prospect Books, 2005).

22   *Is authenticity . . .* Sejal Sukhadwala, "The Bogus Quest for 'Authentic' Food," May 28, 2012, theguardian.com/lifeandstyle/wordofmouth/2012/may/28/bogus-quest-for-authentic
-food. For a discussion, see Michael Steinberger, "Can Anyone Save French Food"; see also Denning, "Authenticity and Italian Food."

22   *What kind of authenticity . . .* Heldke, *Exotic Appetites.*

22   *Who gets to . . .* Sherri Inness has a sensitive and insightful discussion of the problem of authenticity in *Secret Ingredients: Race, Gender, and Class at the Dinner Table* (Basingstoke, UK: Palgrave, 2005).

22   *Good cooking requires . . .* Toops, *Eggs*, xv.

22   *gets more authentic . . .* Nicholas F. Silich, "Authentic Food: A Philosophical Approach," in *Authenticity in the Kitchen: Proceedings of the Oxford Symposium on Food and Cookery*, 401–2.

22   *Man's real work . . .* Robert Farrar Capon, *The Supper of the Lamb: A Culinary Reflection* (New York: Modern Library, 2002), 19–20.

22   *American reference . . .* "Omelet vs. Omelette," 2009, grammarist.com/spelling/omelet-omelette/.

23   *When I use . . .* Lewis Carroll, *Through the Looking-Glass* (London: Macmillan and Company, 1934), 205.

23   *Some genealogies . . .* Apicius, *A Critical Edition with an Introduction and English Translation*, trans. Christopher Grocock, ed. C. W. Grocock, Sally Grainger (London: Prospect Books, 2006).

23   overmele: Toops, *Eggs*, 38, 141n3.

24   Le Ménagier . . . Peter Hertzmann, "Les Omelettes," 2005, hertzmann.com/articles/2005/omelettes/.

24   *A recipe from the 1400s . . .* Toops, *Eggs*, 44.

24   *early recipes . . .* Ibid., 45.

24   *mid-16th century . . .* See, for example, Alan Davidson, *Oxford Companion to Food* (New York: Oxford University Press, 1999), 550, 553.

24   *dusted with powdered . . .* Barbara Ketcham Wheaton, *Savoring the Past: The French Kitchen and Table from 1300 to 1789* (New York: Simon & Schuster, 1983), 53.

24   *recipes for "omelettes" . . .* Maguelonne Toussaint-Samat, *A History of Food*, trans. Anthea Bell, rev. ed. (New York: Wiley-Blackwell, 2009), 326.

25   *O mighty . . .* Quoted in Stewart Lee Alan, *In the Devil's Garden: A Sinful History of Forbidden Food* (New York: Ballantine, 2007). Many cosmologies, including those of Australian Aborigines, some Egyptian, and some pre-Buddhist religious sects in Tibet, have believed that the universe is an egg. In certain cultures, among them Philippine and German, eggs are associated with virility. In some others, however, including parts of Ethiopia and Chad, eggs and omelets are said to be taboo, especially for women.

25   *First, chop . . .* Hacker, "Omelette," 175.

27   *will not make . . .* Rachel Hope Cleves, "The Autobiography of Alice B. Toklas," August 27, 2013, rachelhopecleves.com/2013/08/27/the-autobiography-of-alice-b-toklas/.

27   *omelet of Crevecoeur:* Alexandre Dumas, *Twenty Years After* (New York: Oxford, 2009), 87.

27   *Omelette Voltaire:* "If God did not exist, it would be necessary to invent him." Voltaire, *Épître à l'Auteur du Livre des Trois Imposteurs* (1770). Although he is not immortalized in an omelet, Friedrich Nietzsche ("God is dead"), we know, liked to eat them with apple jam. Julian Young, *Friedrich Nietzsche: A Philosophical Biography* (Cambridge, UK: Cambridge University Press, 2010), 456.

28   *could turn . . .* Toussaint-Samat, *A History of Food*, 326.

28   *October 4 . . .* Marty Davis, "The Jean-Paul Sartre Cookbook," pvspade.com/Sartre/cookbook.html.

29   *Brillat-Savarin, however . . .* For a discussion of Brillat-Savarin's philosophy of taste, see Thomas M. Kavanaugh, "Epicureanism Across the French Revolution," in *Lucretius and Modernity: Epicurean Encounters Across Time and Disciplines*, ed. Jacques Lezra and Liza Blake (New York: Palgrave Macmillan, 2016).

29   *a small, unpretentious . . .* P. G. Wodehouse, *A Damsel in Distress* (Aukland: The Floating Press, 2003), 338.

29   *delightful omelette . . .* Willa Cather, *Alexander's Bridge* (Boston: Houghton Mifflin Company, 1992), 67.

29 *You don't know . . .* [etc.]: Garrison Keillor, "Omelette Script," March 1, 2008, prairiehome
.publicradio.org/programs/2008/03/01/scripts/omelette.shtml.

30 *favorite of James . . .* François Rysavy, *A Treasury of White House Cooking* (New York: Putnam, 1972), 154.

30 *perfect plain omelet . . .* [etc.]: Marquis de Sade, *The 120 Days of Sodom and Other Writings* (New York: Grove Press, 1994), 612.

31 *Art should be . . .* Eric Scheie, "De gustibus est disputandum!," January 18, 2007, daliblog
.com/. For references to Dalí's omelet attire, see "Salvador Dalí: Pink Ink to Autograph an
Omelet," *New London Day*, April 12, 1981, 24, news.google.com/newspapers?nid=1915&dat
=19810402&id=XQEhAAAAIBAJ&sjid=_nQFAAAAIBAJ&pg=1049,365743&hl=en.

31 *Chop together . . .* Filippo Tommaso Marinetti, *The Futurist Cookbook*, trans. Suzanne Brill (London: Trefoil Publications, 1989), 144.

31 *An omelet can indeed . . .* For a general discussion about food, art, and aesthetics, see Michelle
Delville, *Food, Poetry, and the Aesthetics of Consumption: Eating the Avant-Garde* (Abingdon, UK: Routledge, 2012).

32 *Picasso . . .* Mary Ann Caws, *The Modern Art Cookbook* (London: Reaktion, 2013), reviewed in
Maria Popova, "The Modern Art Cookbook: Recipes and Food-Inspired Treasures from
the Twentieth Century's Greatest Creative Icons," May 8, 2014, www.brainpickings.
org/2014/05/08/modern-art-cookbook-caws/.

32 *Claude Monet's . . .* Claire Joyes, *Monet's Table: The Cooking Journals of Claude Monet* (New York: Simon
and Schuster, 1989), 171.

32 *I can't make . . .* Danica, "Cooking & Eating à la Garbo," 2005, http://www.garboforever
.com/Cooking_and_eating.htmwww.garboforever.com/Cooking_and_eating.htm.

33 *all sorts . . .* Most political scientists view such topics with practiced disdain. I am happy to
report, though, that some social scientists do indeed take the study of food in the movies
seriously. One of the best works is by Anne L. Bower, *Reel Food: Essays on Food and Film* (Abingdon,
UK: Routledge, 2004). See also the fine work by James R. Keller, *Food, Film, and Culture: A Genre
Study* (Jefferson, NC: McFarland, 2006) and Cynthia Baron et al., *Appetites and Anxieties: Food,
Film, and the Politics of Representation* (Wichita, KS: Wayne State Press, 2013). More generally, see
Steve Zimmerman, *Food in the Movies*, 2nd ed. (Jefferson, NC: McFarland, 2009).

33 *The brothers, the bread . . .* I call it an omelet, but Stanley Tucci says it is a frittata in his cookbook *The
Tucci Table* (New York: Gallery Books, 2014), 31. Tucci writes, "it was crucial that I learned to
make the frittata properly. . . . It is necessary that you have the right pan, by which I mean one
that you feel comfortable with, and the best eggs you can lay your hands on."

34 *I have found none . . .* Madame Romaine de Lyon's wonderful little book on omelets includes
"Some Notes on Omelette Eaters," but is closer to anthropology than to philosophy. *The Art
of Cooking Omelettes*, 148–56.

34 *No detail is . . .* Mary Ann Caws, *The Modern Art Cookbook* (London: Reaktion Books, 2013), 17.

34 *Delight in the act . . .* [etc.]: Capon, *The Supper of the Lamb*, 8.

34 *eat to give . . .* [etc.]: Ibid., 188–89.

34 *with somebody . . .* Hacker, "Omelette," 176.

35 *in America . . .* Lyon, *The Art of Cooking Omelettes*, 152.

35 *It is the experience . . .* Ciardi, *How Does a Poem Mean?*

35 *One cannot get . . .* John E. Finn, "Rumination: How Does a Recipe Mean," February 2, 2016,
tablematters.com/2016/02/17/how-does-a-recipe-mean/.

35 *school of fixed . . .* Ciardi, *How Does a Poem Mean?*

35 *The way to cook . . .* Julia Child, *The Way to Cook* (New York: Alfred A. Knopf, 1989).

36 *All that life offers any . . .* Oliver Wendell Holmes Jr., "The Profession of the Law," in *The Essential
Holmes: Selections from the Letters, Speeches, Judicial Opinions and Other Writings of Oliver Wendell Holmes, Jr.*,
ed. Richard A. Posner (Chicago: University of Chicago Press, 1992), 219.

36 *an omelet is not* . . . Capon, *The Supper of the Lamb*, 123.

38 *Some writers think* . . . Jeffrey Feinman, *The Fabulous Egg Cookbook* (New York: Ventura Associates, 1979), 70.

38 *There are no secrets* . . . Richard Olney, *Simple French Food* (New York: Wiley, 1992).

38 *no clever arrangement* . . . William O'Flaherty, "Bad Eggs," December 19, 2015, www.essentialcslewis .com/2015/12/19/ccslq-16-bad-eggs/.

38 *M. F. K. Fisher* . . . M. F. K. Fisher, "How Not to Boil an Egg," in *How to Cook a Wolf* (New York: Macmillan Press, 1988), 53.

39 *if they want to:* With apologies to the B-52s. "Roam," *Cosmic Thing* (Reprise Records, 1989).

40 *Hold in front* . . . Fannie Farmer, *The Boston Cooking-School Cook Book* (New York: Little, Brown & Company, 1911), 95.

41 *Apply the tongue* . . . Isabella Beeton, *Mrs. Beeton's Book of Household Management*, 3rd ed. (New York: 1977), 823.

41 *which came first:* Diane Toops tells us that the current state of scientific knowledge is that the egg came first, citing a study by a team made up of a scientist from the University of Nottingham, a philosopher at King's College, and a poultry farmer. Toops, *Eggs*, 96–97.

41 *eggs as an object* . . . Indeed, before there were humans, or chickens, for that matter, there were certainly eggs. As Harold McGee notes, "Eggs . . . are millions of years older than birds. . . . The first eggs were released, fertilized, and hatched in the ocean. Around 250 million years ago, the earliest fully land-dwelling animals, the reptiles, developed a self-contained egg with a tough, leathery skin. . . ." Harold McGee, *On Food and Cooking: The Science and Lore of the Kitchen* (New York: Simon & Schuster, 1984), 55, 69–70.

41 *Bird eggs appeared* . . . Ibid., 69–70.

41 *A hen is only* . . . Samuel Butler, *Life and Habit* (Trubner: 1878), 134.

41 *development of domesticated* . . . Toops, *Eggs*, 33–34.

41 *Egyptians ate eggs* . . . Ibid., 35.

42 *in 2015* . . . American Egg Board, "About the US Egg Industry," August 8, 2016, aeb.org/ farmers-and-marketers/industry-overview.

42 *in 1945* . . . Roberto A. Ferdman, "Americans Once Ate Nearly Twice as Many Eggs as They do Today," April 2, 2014, qz.com/194070/americans-once-ate-nearly-twice-as-many-eggs -as-they-do-today/.

42 *A recent study* . . . Kristen Domonell, "How to Reduce Your Caloric Intake by 30%," April 13, 2016, www.cnn.com/2016/04/13/health/how-to-eat-fewer-calories/index.html.

43 *favored by 88 percent* . . . Mintel, "Egg Market Shows No Signs of Cracking," June 24, 2011, mintel.com/press-centre/food-and-drink/egg-market-shows-no-signs-of-cracking.

43 *nature's perfect food:* Yes, there was. American Egg Board, 2006, www.aeb.org/images/ website/documents/food-manufacturers/order-aeb-resources/Egg_Products_Reference_ Guide.pdf.

43 *A single large* . . . Jennifer Trainer Thompson, *The Fresh Egg Cookbook: From Chicken to Kitchen* (North Adams, MA: Storey Press, 2012), 2.

44 *Fresh eggs have* . . . Ibid., 7. See also Ruhlman, *Egg*, xvii.

44 *Eggs were said* . . . Select Committee on Nutrition and Human Needs, US Senate, "Dietary Goals for the United States," (Washington, DC, 1977).

44 *in 2015* . . . Jen Christensen, "New U.S. Dietary Guidelines Limit Sugar, Rethink Cholesterol," January 7, 2016, cnn.com/2016/01/07/health/2015-dietary-guidelines/index.html.

44 *Egg yolks, low* . . . Toops, *Eggs*, 56. Indeed, eggs have received a perfect 1.0 score on the Protein Digestibility Corrected Amino Acid Score.

45 *cooking reduces* . . . Centers for Disease Control and Prevention, "Salmonella and Eggs," May 25, 2016, cdc.gov/features/salmonellaeggs/.

45   Fresh grade A . . . McGee, On Food and Cooking, 62–63.

45   about 55 grams: Ibid.

48   The ancient Chinese . . . Toops, Eggs, 109.

48   may be bought . . . [etc.]: Farmer, The Boston Cooking-School Cook Book, 95.

49   But cracking . . . Amusingly, there is a very fine book, compiled by the editors of Fine Cooking magazine, entitled How to Break an Egg: 1,453 Kitchen Tips, Food Fixes, Emergency Substitutions, and Handy Techniques (Newtown, CT: Taunton Press, 2005). I find the title amusing because not a one of the over 1,400 handy kitchen tips actually tells us how to break an egg!

49   which tends to push . . . Jacques Pépin, La Technique: An Illustrated Guide to the Fundamental Techniques of Cooking (New York: Times Books, 1976).

49   you cannot break . . . Toops, Eggs, 23–24.

50   The current record . . . Ibid., 26.

50   yield pretty much . . . Ruhlman, Egg, xv.

50   Any man . . . Capon, The Supper of the Lamb, 123.

52   With time, some . . . Alina Tugend, "How Not to Wreck a Nonstick Pan," December 17, 2010, www.nytimes.com/2010/12/18/your-money/18shortcuts.html?_r=1.

53   to most Americans . . . David Rosengarten, Taste: One Palate's Journey Through the World's Greatest Dishes (New York: Random House, 1998), 119.

54   The key . . . Anne Willan, Cook it Right: Achieve Perfection with Every Dish You Cook (Pleasantville, PA: Reader's Digest, 1997), 98.

54   must have a pan . . . Dione Lucas and Marion Gorman, The Dione Lucas Book of French Cooking (Boston: Little, Brown, 1947), 209.

55   some pans are hedgehogs . . . Isaiah Berlin, The Hedgehog and the Fox: An Essay on Tolstoy's View of History (London: Weidenfeld & Nicolson, 1953).

55   philosophy of symmetry . . . Most contemporary uses of symmetry are in the philosophy of science and contemporary physics. For a good introduction, see "Symmetry and Symmetry Breaking," Stanford Encyclopedia of Philosophy, plato.stanford.edu/entries/symmetry-breaking/.

55   Omelette pans generate . . . Irma S. Rombauer and Marion Rombauer Becker, The Joy of Cooking (New York: Macmillan, 1975), 226.

57   by "favorite" . . . David Sutton and Michael Hernandez, "Voices in the Kitchen: Cooking Tools as an Inalienable Possessions," Oral History 67 (2007), www.academia.edu/2157630/ Voices_in_the_Kitchen_Cooking_Tools_as_Inalienable_Possessions.

58   We found that . . . OXO Good Grips Flip and Fold Omelet Turner, www.amazon.de/ Omelet-Turner-Haus-Garten-Wartung/dp/B00J0AJ94O.

59   [Tending] implies . . . Sheldon Wolin, The Presence of the Past: Essays on the State and the Constitution (Baltimore: Johns Hopkins University Press, 1990), 89. See also Finn, "Rumination."

59   concentration on the present . . . [etc.]: Pierre Hadot, Philosophy as a Way of Life: Spiritual Exercises from Socrates to Foucault (New York: Wiley, 1995), 85.

59   an omelet is . . . Silas Weir, The Guillotine Club: And Other Stories (New York: Century Club, 1910), 5.

61   If you know . . . [etc.]: Ruhlman, Egg, xiii.

61   Play, Plato . . . Gavin Ardley, "The Role of Play in the Philosophy of Plato," Philosophy 42 (1967), 226–42.

62   As the water . . . For a very useful discussion, see J. Kenji López-Alt, The Food Lab: Better Home Cooking Through Science (New York: W. W. Norton, 2015), 117–18.

63   eggs seem to . . . Narcissa Chamberlain, The Omelette Book (New York: David R. Godine, 2009), 15.

63   will be firm . . . Quoted in Lucas and Gorman, The Dione Lucas Book of French Cooking, 207. This book includes a wonderful compendium of quotations from famous chefs and food writers about the mysteries of the omelet.

67   *Frittatas . . . require . . .* Michelle Maisto, *The Gastronomy of Marriage: A Memoir of Food and Love* (New York: Random House, 2009), 215.

67   *fat, which discourages . . .* At least, this is J. Kenji López-Alt's explanation. Makes sense to me. . . . López-Alt, *The Food Lab,* 118.

70   *the apprehensive . . .* Richard Olney, *Simple French Food* (New York: Houghton-Mifflin Harcourt, 2014), 87.

70   *I have given . . .* Quoted in Toops, *Eggs,* 51.

70   *tightrope walker . . .* Karen Abbot, "The Daredevil of Niagara Falls," *Smithsonian Magazine,* October 18, 2011, www.smithsonianmag.com/history/the-daredevil-of-niagara-falls-110492884/?no-ist.

71   *To this day . . .* Claude Quétel, *Le Mont-Saint-Michel* (Paris: Bordas, 1991).

71   *a dry and tasteless . . .* Chamberlain, *The Omelette Book,* 21.

71   *I understand . . .* Similarly, soufflé omelets were a marker of social status and class, as revealed in this extract from a story by Howard Hazeltine published in 1886. In "The Wife's Secret," Hazeltine establishes his middle-class standing by noting, among other things, "Our cook cannot compass an omelette soufflée." [*sic*]. "The Wife's Secret," *Ballou's Monthly Magazine* 64 (July 1886), 273–278.

76   *Hell is . . .* There is some doubt about whether Sartre actually said this, but if he didn't, I'm sure he meant to. Craig Silverman, "New York Times Correction: Hell is *Not* Other People at Breakfast," March 28, 2012, poynter.org/2012/new-york-times-correction-hell-is-not -other-people-at-breakfast/167876/.

80   *Marjorie's Mosser's . . .* Marjorie Mosser, *Good Maine Food: Ancient and Modern New England Food & Drink* (Camden: Down East Books, 2010), 228.

82   *including James Beard . . .* James Beard, *American Cookery* (New York: Little, Brown, 2009), 109–110.

94   *That's no omelette . . .* Pierre Franey, *A Chef's Tale: A Memoir of France, Food and America* (Lincoln: Bison Books, 2010), 47–48.

108   *very slowly, to allow . . .* Elizabeth David, *French Provincial Cooking* (New York: Penguin Books, 1999), 114.

110   *Lady Caroline . . .* Oscar Wilde, *A Woman of No Importance* (1893), at Project Gutenberg, Oscar Wilde, "A Woman of No Importance," gutenberg.org/files/854/854-h/854-h.htm.

110   *much depends . . .* Margaret Visser, *Much Depends on Dinner: The Extraordinary History and Mythology, Allure and Obsessions, Perils and Taboos of an Ordinary Meal* (New York: Grove/Atlantic, 2010). The original quotation is from *The Island,* by Lord George Gordon Byron: "All human history attests That happiness for man, / the hungry sinner! / Since Eve ate apples, much depends on dinner." (1823, at archive.org/details/islandorchristia02byro.

150   *Some scholars . . .* Alan Davidson, *Oxford Companion to Food* (New York: Oxford University Press, 1999), 553.

151   *The trail . . .* Ibid.

151   *Egg Foyung:* Marjorie Mills, *Better Homes Recipe Book* (Boston: Herald-Traveler, 1933), under a section entitled "a Chinese thought on eggs," includes a recipe for "Eggs Foyung," 50.

166   *a slightly larger . . .* Gole, "Olé, Omelette."

186   *Claudia Roden . . .* Claudia Roden, *The New Book of Middle Eastern Food* (New York: Alfred A. Knopf, 2000), 173.

187   *Maacouda bi Batata . . .* Ibid.

190   *With the general . . .* August Escoffier, *The Escoffier Cook Book: A Guide to the Fine Art of Cookery* (New York: Crown, 1941), 761.

190   *With the aid . . .* Adolphe Meyer, *Eggs in a Thousand Ways: A Guide for the Preparation of Eggs for the Table* (New York: Hotel Monthly Press, 1917), 109.

190   *Omelette surprise Pompadour* . . . Rysavy, *A Treasury of White House Cooking*, 154.

191   *the roots of Baked* . . . Bill Grantham, "Review: Brilliant Mischief: The French on Anti-Americanism," *World Policy Journal* 20 (2003), 95. Jefferson's presentation of the dish may have been designed to tweak "One of the leading traitors of the American Revolution," Benjamin Thompson (Count Rumford), a Loyalist who absconded to Paris after the war and spent the remainder of his life investigating the scientific properties of heat. In the process, Rumford devised a recipe for something very much like Basked Alaska. See John Mariani, *The Dictionary of American Food and Drink*, 2nd ed. (New York: Hearst, 1994).

219   *You can also* . . . Paula Wolfert, *The Cooking of Southwest France: Recipes from France's Magnificent Rustic Cuisine* (New York: John Wiley and Sons, 2005), 368.

Index

---◦─◉─◦---